Cambridge Elements ≡

Religion and Monotheism
edited by
Chad Meister
Bethel University
Paul K. Moser
Loyola University Chicago

MONOTHEISM AND CONTEMPORARY ATHEISM

Michael Ruse
Florida State University

CAMBRIDGE
UNIVERSITY PRESS

CAMBRIDGE
UNIVERSITY PRESS

University Printing House, Cambridge CB2 8BS, United Kingdom

One Liberty Plaza, 20th Floor, New York, NY 10006, USA

477 Williamstown Road, Port Melbourne, VIC 3207, Australia

314–321, 3rd Floor, Plot 3, Splendor Forum, Jasola District Centre,
New Delhi – 110025, India

79 Anson Road, #06–04/06, Singapore 079906

Cambridge University Press is part of the University of Cambridge.

It furthers the University's mission by disseminating knowledge in the pursuit of
education, learning, and research at the highest international levels of excellence.

www.cambridge.org
Information on this title: www.cambridge.org/9781108731492
DOI: 10.1017/9781108758635

First published 2019

A catalogue record for this publication is available from the British Library.

ISBN 978-1-108-73149-2 Paperback
ISSN 2631-3014 (online)
ISSN 2631-3006 (print)

Monotheism and Contemporary Atheism

Religion and Monotheism

DOI: 9781108758635
First published online: August 2019

Michael Ruse
Florida State University

Author for correspondence: Michael Ruse, mruse@fsu.edu

Abstract: In this Element, Michael Ruse offers a critical analysis of contemporary atheism. He puts special emphasis on the work of so-called New Atheists: Richard Dawkins, Sam Harris, Daniel Dennett, and Christopher Hitchins, whose views are contrasted with those of Edward O. Wilson. Ruse also provides a full exposition of his own position, which he labels "Darwinian existentialism."

Keywords: Darwin, atheism, Richard Dawkins, Darwinian existentialism, Sam Harris, New Atheism

ISBNs: 9781108731492 (PB), 9781108758635 (OC)
ISSNs: 2631-3014 (online), 2631-3006 (print)

Contents

Prologue

"The God of the Old Testament is arguably the most unpleasant character in all fiction: jealous and proud of it; a petty, unjust, unforgiving control-freak; a vindictive, bloodthirsty ethnic cleanser; a misogynistic, homophobic, racist, infanticidal, genocidal, filicidal, pestilential, megalomaniacal, sadomasochistic, capriciously malevolent bully." Thus read the opening lines of Richard Dawkins's runaway bestseller, *The God Delusion* (2006). A lot could be said – will be said – about this passage and the many pages that follow. Here, now, I want to point out that this is not really an epistemological statement – that is, a statement about the truth of things – but overwhelmingly an ethical statement – a statement about the morality of the situation. Whether or not God exists, He is a Very Bad Thing. The pressure is on us not to believe in Him. Rejection of God-belief for people like Dawkins – atheism – is never purely a matter of fact. It is always primarily a matter of right and wrong, of good and evil.

You might say that this cannot be so. Whether or not God exists cannot normally be a matter of morality, even though obviously it can be if He does exist and you wantonly reject Him and His being. Richard Dawkins exists, and that is a fact. Spiderman does not exist, and that is a fact. Either God exists, or He doesn't. End of argument. Things, however, are never quite this simple. Even the most confirmed believers admit that doubts are possible. Indeed, sometimes it is the most confirmed believers who are wracked by doubts. How so? Because God being God you can never be quite sure. Many Christians make something of this. For Søren Kierkegaard, faith had to involve a leap into the absurd in some sense. A God who could be proven once and for all precludes genuine faith, that sense of commitment, of trusting, of being led in the dark.

The famous British review *Beyond the Fringe* had one of the characters (played by Alan Bennett) as a vicar giving a farcical sermon about the nature of existence. "Life, you know, is rather like opening a tin of sardines. We are all of us looking for the key. And, I wonder, how many of you here tonight have wasted years of your lives looking behind the kitchen dressers of this life for that key." He continues: "Others think they've found the key, don't they? They roll back the lid of the sardine tin of life, they reveal the sardines, the riches of life, therein, and they get them out, they enjoy them. But, you know, there's always a little bit in the corner you can't get out. I wonder – I wonder, is there a little bit in the corner of your life? I know there is in mine." What makes this so hilarious is that it is not exactly false. Substitute "God" for "life" and there is always that little bit in the corner you can't get out. God's existence – or nonexistence – is always tantalizingly at a distance, and that means commitment, and that means morality.

Belief in the existence of God. Right or wrong? Good or bad? This is the theme of this short Element. I set these questions against the fact that, in this century, we have seen a surprisingly large wave of God deniers – the so-called New Atheists. My aim is to look at these earnest thinkers – preachers or proselytizers are terms that come to mind – to put them in context and to see what they are saying. Then I seek to assess the strengths of their arguments – to see the good points, to see the bad points, and to draw conclusions. Some commentators on this controversy have objected that even to set about things in this way is implicitly to give the game to the critics (Crane 2017). Religion is about far more than belief – or not – in God, or even in the moral consequences that follow from such beliefs. Religion is about rituals and customs and identi-fication with one group rather than another. In short, religion is about the whole lived life. To focus just on God is to distort the discussion from the first. I agree that religion is more than just beliefs or not in a deity, but I think the critics are right in assuming that such beliefs are at the heart of religion. For me, for instance, raised a Quaker, rituals have never been much a part of religion. So, without prejudging issues too strongly, I am with the critics in my focusing on the God and morality issues.

As it happens, though this Elements series is on "monotheism" generally, rather than on "Christian monotheism" specifically, simply because of the interests of the New Atheists – those whom they berate first and foremost – my chief (my default) focus is on Christian monotheism, only as appropriate broadening my discussion. I refer therefore to the God of both the Old and New Testaments, to God the Father, and His extensions through the Trinity – His son, Jesus Christ, and the Holy Ghost or Spirit. He is the creator and ruler of the universe, ever-present, loving all but especially those beings made in His own image, human beings.

In what I take to be entirely standard usage, since we are now referring (for all that He is three-in-one) to one and only one God, I speak of belief in this God as "theism" with the associated term "theistic" (Ruse 2015). A God who did not create but who ordered and designed the universe is the God of "deism" and such beliefs are "deistic." The main difference between the God of theism – the Creator God – and the God of deism – the Unmoved Mover – is that the former continues (or can continue) to interfere in the world's working through miracles. The latter cannot (or does not). Nonbelief starts with what Thomas Henry Huxley labeled "agnosticism." You simply don't know whether God exists or not. For some, agnosticism simply marks their total lack of interest in the topic. They don't care whether God exists. Others, like T. H. Huxley's grandson Julian

Huxley, care very much. They are in this sense deeply religious. Julian Huxley wrote a book: *Religion without Revelation* (1927). A better term for these religious nonbelievers might be "skeptic." At the end of the spectrum, you have those who assert the nonexistence of God as firmly as theists assert the existence of God. These are "atheists."

These terms help our discussion. They are essential. But be warned, there are always queries and qualifications. Buddhists are neither theists nor deists – they do not believe in a Creator or Designer God. In respects, though, they are as far from agnosticism and atheism as it is possible to imagine (Ruse 2019). They believe in orders of lesser gods and their whole world is as infused with meaning as one finds in any Abrahamic religion, especially the Christian religion. It would be as misleading to refer without qualification to the Dalai Lama as an atheist as it would be to refer to Pope Francis as an atheist. Quakers reject the God of an evangelical like Franklin Graham as firmly as would Richard Dawkins. Does that therefore mean that Quakers are atheists? Or that, as did the followers of Baal, Franklin Graham is following a false God? Questions like these, and the difficulty of answering them, show that the God debate moves on from simple epistemological questions to ethical questions, and these ethical questions take us right into issues to do with meaning. A major reason why most of us would feel uncomfortable simply dismissing Buddhists as atheists, in the same category as Richard Dawkins, and equally uncomfortable with sneering at Quakers for their nigh-mystical approach to the Godhead, is that, unlike Dawkins, these people find an external – an objective – meaning to their lives. Differing from French novelist and essayist Albert Camus ([1942]1955), they do not think their lives "absurd," something William Shakespeare captured in *Macbeth* centuries ago.

> Life's but a walking shadow, a poor player,
> That struts and frets his hour upon the stage,
> And then is heard no more. It is a tale
> Told by an idiot, full of sound and fury,
> Signifying nothing.

For those who reject atheism (and probably most forms of agnosticism), human life makes sense, a sense that is given to us and not created by us in the fashion promoted by the existentialists. So here is another reason – perhaps the most important reason – for careful use of the categories of religious belief.

In hallowed philosophical fashion, cautioning about our use of words, I have stirred the language pot. Mischief over, I am ready to begin. First, some historical background and context. Then the New Atheists. We can take things from there.

1 Why Atheism?

Athens and Jerusalem

Famously, the early Christian thinker Tertullian (AD 155–240) asked: "What has Athens to do with Jerusalem?" He was arguing that the Christian faith should avoid the snares of the false pagan philosophy of the Greeks – Plato and Aristotle, particularly. Later Christian thinkers, above all Augustine and Aquinas, were to disagree strongly with this position, but they (as do we) agreed with Tertullian that it is to Greek and to Jewish thought – seen in harmony or seen in opposition – that we turn to discover the nature of Christian monotheism, and even more to discover the nature of (let us use the oxymoron) Christian atheism. In respects, it does seem that Tertullian has a point. Nonbelief simply does not come as an option in either the Jewish contribution to the Bible, the Old Testament, or the Christian Bible, the New Testament. "The fool hath said in his heart there is no God." Although Anselm quoted this passage from the Psalms (14:1), stating his case for the ontological argument, general agreement is that this was not truly an avowal of nonbelief. Rather, it was a denial of the God of the Jews. There were lots of people like that – the already mentioned followers of Baal, for example. And there was certainly much hostility to the devotees of alien deities. But there was no atheism, or even agnosticism, in the senses we are using the words.

Why was this? To get at God, as it were, there seem to be two paths. On one hand is the path introduced in the Prologue – that of faith, meaning that, in some sense, psychologically you are overwhelmed by the conviction of God's existence like Saul on the road to Damascus. On the other hand is the path Anselm is about to pursue, where you try to use reason and evidence to prove the existence of God. Using the conventional terms of "revealed theology" (meaning belief on faith) and "natural theology" (meaning belief on reason and evidence), there is very little of the latter in any part of the Bible. Exceptionally, in the Psalms we learn: "The heavens declare the glory of God; and the firmament sheweth his handywork" (19:1). Passages elsewhere, notably Paul speaking in the Areopagus (Acts 17), reveal hints of natural theological reasoning. Generally, the very attempt to prove (or deny) the existence of God gets short shrift. The Jews were not into that sort of thing. It was faith or nothing, and nothing was not an option. Jesus made that clear. "Then saith he to Thomas, reach hither thy finger, and behold my hands; and reach hither thy hand, and thrust it into my side: and be not faithless, but believing. And Thomas answered and said unto him, My Lord and my God. Jesus saith unto him, Thomas, because thou hast seen me, thou hast believed: blessed are they that have not seen, and yet have believed" (John 20:27–29).

In the spirit of this kind of thinking, as noted in the Prologue, belief in the existence of God is always somewhat at a distance, that little bit in the corner that you can't get out. It is obviously true that many people of faith don't have this worry – "I know that my redeemer liveth, and that he shall stand at the latter day upon the earth" (Job 19:25) – but it is equally obviously true that many people do have doubts and sincere believers can wrestle with these throughout their lives. Indeed, paradoxically, it can be that which makes faith so vital. Followers of natural theology would tend to disagree. They would argue that reason and evidence can prove definitively the existence of God. You can empty all the corners. "God exists" is true or not true. Forget all the worries about morality and meaning.

Faith and Reason

To answer this sturdy argument, three points are pertinent.

First, in the Christian tradition, faith has always trumped reason and evidence. With reason, Thomas Aquinas is taken to be the greatest natural theologian of all time. Yet he makes no bones about where he stands on the faith/reason divide. "The truth of the intelligible things of God is twofold, one to which the inquiry of reason can attain, the other which surpasses the whole range of human reason" (Aquinas 1975, 7). Aquinas asserts definitively that faith is the more important – else the ignorant and stupid and lazy would never get knowledge of God. The recent pope Saint John Paul II stood right in this tradition: "The results of reasoning may in fact be true, but these results acquire their true meaning only if they are set within the larger horizon of faith: 'All man's steps are ordered by the Lord: how then can man understand his own ways?' [Proverbs 20:24]" (John Paul II 1998, 16).

Second, the natural-theological proofs may be found wanting. This is a major item discussed in this Element. Full knowledge of God may not be so easily available as you first thought. Note that, here, revealed theology is in a somewhat stronger position. The critic can go after revealed theology, for instance arguing that it is all a matter of psychology, wishful thinking, and belief in God has no stronger basis than belief in winning the lottery. This is true, but that is hardly going to stop the believer from believing. After all, he or she has already foresworn reason and evidence, so reason and evidence are not going to be definitively effective now. In any case, by next week you may know that you did not win the lottery. God-belief will only be authenticated after death, when there is going to be no one around to laugh at you for your naivety.

Third, if you do go the route of natural theology, then you open the path to atheism. The person of belief might turn from God because of the horrors of the

Holocaust. But you certainly cannot make them turn from God because of the Holocaust, and it is as likely that they will reaffirm their belief in the Christian God because of the Holocaust. Only in the overall Christian eschatological scheme of things can one make sense of the Holocaust. Don't mistake me. I am not trying to slide in at the beginning of this Element that that makes Christians horrible people. I don't see that as necessarily or universally true at all. What I am saying is that the Holocaust for a person of faith is not the knockdown argument that a black swan is to the biologist who believes that all swans are white. I am also saying that if you go the route of natural theology – reason and evidence – then you do open yourself to refutations for the existence of God. Nothing in the corners of the tin to shield you. So atheism is now firmly on the table.

The Greeks

As it was for the Greeks in a way not true for the Jews. Neither Plato nor Aristotle was an atheist. They certainly knew of atheists and Plato for one disapproved of them. He wanted them locked up, fed only by slaves, and buried outside the city walls. Talk about a moral issue! This is about on a par with being a child abuser. Although neither Plato nor Aristotle was given to dancing around stark naked ("skyclad") or cutting the sacred mistletoe or calling down the moon, in the sense of pagan as someone outside the Abrahamic religions, that is obviously where they fall. Neither was into the polytheism we associate with ancient Greece – gods on Mount Olympus fighting and copulating and feasting and so forth. Both thought that sort of thing not just wrong but rather common and vulgar. Plato had his Theory of Forms, supposing that there is a rational world of universals or archetypes that our material world copies in some sense – "participates in." Just as our world is ordered, with the sun being the prime force illuminating and giving sustaining existence to all else, so in the world of the Forms the Good is the prime force illuminating and giving sustaining existence to all else. Aristotle likewise had his Unmoved Mover, the totally perfect being toward which all else strives.

There are similarities between Plato's Form of the Good and Aristotle's Unmoved Mover – and incidentally, not contingently, with the Christian God (Ruse 2017). All are outside time and space, perfect, unchanging, and the cause of all else. However, Aristotle's Unmoved Mover does the only thing such a perfect being can do, contemplate perfection, meaning think only of itself (!). It has therefore no knowledge or interest in anything else, certainly not the things of this world. Plato's Good is very different, for it does have concern for the rest of existence – not the rest of creation, for Plato like Aristotle (and very much unlike the Christian) did not think the world was created. It existed always – eternal. However, Plato's Form of the Good was a designer – it was this that made the world (universe) as it is, and it was this that strove to make everything within the world as good as possible. There is debate about whether the Good-as-Designer – what Plato called the "Demiurge" – did an actual act of designing in space and time, or if (as most think) It was more a principle of ordering. Either way, Plato (probably drawing on earlier thinkers, especially Socrates) started the Western tradition of natural theology, for he argued that the design-like nature of our world points to an external intelligence that planned the way that things are and function. The eye, for seeing, did not come about by chance. It was intended to be that way, thanks to the benevolent forethought of the Demiurge. For Plato, all physical existence shows design – inanimate objects as well as organisms – and this was true also of Aristotle. However, given the indifference of the Unmoved Mover – no designer It – the principle of ordering had to be a "vital" force within, rather than an external intelligence. Also, because earlier in life he was a practicing biologist, Aristotle always thought more of functioning – what he spoke of as being guided by "final causes" as opposed to regular "efficient causes" – in the world of organisms than in the whole physical world. Whatever the differences, however, there is not much atheism about Plato and Aristotle.

The Christians

Which makes it hardly unexpected that the great Christian philosophers-theologians, notably Augustine, Anselm, and Aquinas, picked up on essential elements of Greek philosophy and incorporated them right into their world systems (Ruse 2015). Augustine's God bears remarkable similarities to the Platonic Form of the Good, no surprise since he was much influenced by the Neoplatonist Plotinus. In the *Confessions*, Augustine homes right in on the key points. Necessary: "For God's will is not a creature but is prior to the created order, since nothing would be created unless the Creator's will preceded it. Therefore God's will belongs to his very substance." Outside space: "no physical entity existed before heaven and earth." Outside time: "Your 'years' neither come nor go. Our years come and go so that all may come in succession. All your 'years' exist in simultaneity, because they do not change; those going away are not thrust out by those coming in … Your Today is eternity" (Augustine 396, Book XI). In some sense, as with the Good, the Christian God does not exist contingently – like the objects of this world – but necessarily. Hard as it is to imagine, there might indeed have been a world without Michael Ruse. It is impossible that there be a world without God.

This point leads to the most notorious of the proofs of God – the ontological argument of Anselm (1903), which asserts His being straight from His definition. God is defined as "that than which none greater can be conceived." Suppose, with the fool, we say that God does not exist. We run into a reductio ad absurdum. "God cannot be conceived not to exist. – God is that than which nothing greater can be conceived. – That which can be conceived not to exist is not God." In the *Summa*, Aquinas offers a neo-Aristotelian, teleology-drenched picture of all of nature, although he is not at all adverse to using Neoplatonic notions in his thinking too. These emerge particularly in his famous fivefold proofs for the existence of God. First, a series of variations on the causal or cosmological argument for God's existence: everything has a cause, ultimately we are led back to a first cause, namely God. The second version is perhaps the easiest version to grasp:

> In the world of sense we find there is an order of efficient causes. There is no case known (neither is it, indeed, possible) in which a thing is found to be the efficient cause of itself; for so it would be prior to itself, which is impossible. Now in efficient causes it is not possible to go on to infinity, because in all efficient causes following in order, the first is the cause of the intermediate cause, and the intermediate is the cause of the ultimate cause, whether the intermediate cause be several, or only one. Now to take away the cause is to take away the effect. Therefore, if there be no first cause among efficient causes, there will be no ultimate, nor any intermediate cause. But if in efficient causes it is possible to go on to infinity, there will be no first efficient cause, neither will there be an ultimate effect, nor any intermediate efficient causes; all of which is plainly false. Therefore it is necessary to admit a first efficient cause, to which everyone gives the name of God. (Aquinas 1952, 1a, 2, 3)

The fifth argument is a version of Plato's teleological argument, the argument from design.

> We see that things which lack intelligence, such as natural bodies, act for an end, and this is evident from their acting always, or nearly always, in the same way, so as to obtain the best result. Hence it is plain that not fortuitously, but designedly, do they achieve their end. Now whatever lacks intelligence cannot move towards an end, unless it be directed by some being endowed with knowledge and intelligence; as the arrow is shot to its mark by the archer. Therefore some intelligent being exists by whom all natural things are directed to their end; and this being we call God. (Aquinas 1952, 1a, 2, 3)

Notice that, like Augustine and Anselm, Aquinas is assuming that God exists necessarily. He must or we run into the obvious objection: "What caused God?" God for these great thinkers has no cause and has no need of a cause. Obviously, we need to do some more unpacking of this claim. We turn to this task later in this Element. For now, it is enough to state that through a combination of faith and reason – remember, the first was always prior – right through the medieval period the basic, Christian monotheist position made good sense.

Atheism

What then of the atheists who so disturbed Plato? Most notably there were the atomists who argued that the universe is empty space filled with little balls of matter – atoms – that buzzed around aimlessly. Every now and then they collided and stuck together. Gradually over time these chunks of matter got bigger and bigger, and since there was infinite time and space – just like monkeys typing Shakespeare – every now and then something functioning appeared. "Friends, Romans, countrymen." Working ears and eyes. So it all came together, without rhyme or reason, without purpose or intention. Leucippus and his student Democritus (around the fifth century BC) were the early atomists, followed by Plato's contemporary Epicurus (341–270 BC) – who much influenced the Roman poet Lucretius (94–55 BC). His poem *On the Nature of Things* lays out things starkly.

> At that time the earth tried to create many monsters
> with weird appearance and anatomy –
> androgynous, of neither one sex nor the other but
> somewhere in between; some footless, or handless;
> many even without mouths, or without eyes and blind;
> some with their limbs stuck together all along their body,
> and thus disabled from doing harm or obtaining anything
> they needed.
> These and other monsters the earth created.
> But to no avail, since nature prohibited their development.
> They were unable to reach the goal of their maturity,
> to find sustenance or to copulate.

Nothing works. It is a mess. Then, time cures all.

> First, the fierce and savage lion species
> has been protected by its courage, foxes by cunning, deer by
> speed of flight. But as for the light-sleeping
> minds of dogs, with their faithful heart,
> and every kind born of the seed of beasts of burden,
> and along with them the wool-bearing flocks and the
> horned tribes,
> they have all been entrusted to the care of the human race.
>
> (Lucretius 1950, 5.862–867)

Even in offering an alternative, meaningless scenario, Plato and later thinkers saw this kind of thinking as a threat to societal stability. What price ethics and the rule of law when all is simply a matter of chance, without rhyme or reason? Overall, though, the main objection – as Plato makes very clear in the *Phaedo* – is that it is all so implausible. It is all very well to talk about infinite time and space – who can grasp those concepts? In the real world, Murphy's Law prevails – if it can go wrong, it will go wrong. Piles of junk simply don't jump up and start functioning. They just don't.

The Modern Age

What changed things? There were no New Atheists in the Middle Ages. Why do we have them now? Essentially, we have them because of the Three Rs: the Renaissance, the Reformation, and the (Scientific) Revolution (Ruse 2019). The Renaissance brought a renewal of interest in the writings of the ancients. Works like *On the Nature of Things* had a whole new life and an eager audience. This did not mean that people at once became atheists, but the option was being presented anew. Similarly, the Reformation, the break with the Catholic Church by Luther and Calvin and others, hardly signaled a turn to nonbelief. If anything, the Reformers were more ardently Christian than the Catholic establishment. But the differences in beliefs and practices showed the way to thinking outside the loop, and this pointed the way to the possibilities of little or no belief at all. Finally, the Scientific Revolution was no clarion call to atheism. Copernicus, at the beginning, was a minor cleric who died in good standing. Newton, at the end, was deeply religious, in later life spending far more time on biblical interpretation than on physics. It did, however, put the sun at the center of things, rather downgrading the special status of things on Earth, and, more important, it challenged Aristotelian final causes. Rather than thinking of the universe in organic terms, the new breed of scientists thought in mechanical terms, of the world as a machine.

Of course, machines have purposes, but that part of the metaphor (in the physical sciences, at least) was downgraded and dropped. The new science simply thought of the world as in endless motion, governed by blind laws. God could still exist, but He was pushed out of scientific explanation. In the words of one of the greatest historians of the Scientific Revolution, He became "a retired engineer" (Dijksterhuis 1961, 491). It is significant that, for all his religiosity, Newton moved toward a form of deism, denying the Trinity, and thinking in terms of a world where God no longer interferes. This was the pattern set through the eighteenth century. Benjamin Franklin, for instance, was open about all of this. "Some Books against Deism fell into my Hands; they were said to be the Substance of Sermons preached at Boyle's Lectures. It happened that they wrought an Effect on me quite contrary to what was intended by them: For the Arguments of the Deists which were quoted to be refuted, appeared to me much Stronger than the Refutations. In short I soon became a thorough Deist" (2009, 58).

Note that this is deism, not agnosticism or atheism. And this, despite that through the eighteenth century, people like David Hume hammered away at the natural theological arguments for God's existence – especially the argument from design – and as we entered the nineteenth century, people (especially German scholars) were attacking the foundations of revealed theology. So-called higher criticism looked at the books of the Bible as though they were humanly written documents, and quickly and thoroughly they started to fall apart as authentically divine narratives. They appeared much more likely the parables and tales of people long ago, who wrote down these fables and then through traditional retelling considered them divinely inspired. The fly in the ointment, however, if we might be allowed an appropriate metaphor, was the world of organisms. They just didn't seem to be the products of blind laws. They were teleological, bound by final causes, and to one and all – theist and deist – this meant a Designer.

Robert Boyle, the physicist and philosopher, wrestled with this. In the material world, he was a hard-line mechanist. The world works as does the marvelous clock in Strasbourg, where little figures and so forth go through motions on the hour. Organisms, however, seem to call for something more. "Though bats be looked upon as a contemptible sort of creatures, yet I think they may afford us no contemptible argument to our present purpose" ([1688]1966, 194). Boyle pointed to all sorts of adaptations they possess, including the "dugs, to give such to her young ones" (196). Continuing: "Surely by no chance, the female has two teats, unlike the cow, for instance, because that is the number of offspring she has." When it comes to the organic world, we must bring in God, even though we must admit that this is no scientific answer. For most, this was an uneasy compromise, but a workable compromise nevertheless. Indeed, natural theology flourished as never before, reaching its climax in the textbooks written by Archdeacon William Paley of Carlisle. His *Natural Theology* published in 1802 made much of the analogy of the telescope and the eye. As the former was clearly designed and made with a purpose, for seeing, so likewise the eye was designed and made with a purpose, all thanks to the Great Optician in the Sky. What would it mean to deny such a conclusion as this? "This is atheism."

Natural Selection

It was Charles Darwin, in his *Origin of Species* published in 1859, who threw a bomb into all of this (Ruse 1979). A convinced evolutionist after a five-year voyage around the world on HMS *Beagle*, he was also a Cambridge University graduate who had been fed a steady diet of Paley. He knew of and was completely convinced of the design-like nature of organic features, what he called "contrivances" or "adaptations." The question was to find a natural – blind-law-governed – solution. This he found in an equivalent to the selection that breeders practice to produce fleecier sheep and meatier cows and more beautiful and melodious birds. They pick from the best and breed only from them. Darwin quoted an eminent practitioner of the art: "It would seem as if they had chalked out upon a wall a form perfect in itself, and then had given it existence" (Darwin 1859, 31). In nature, argued Darwin, the key lies in the ongoing population pressures made much of by political economist Thomas Robert Malthus. More organisms are born than can survive and reproduce. Available space and food sets limits. There will therefore be a "struggle for existence," and even more a struggle for reproduction. Apparently new variations are always appearing in natural populations – not uncaused but not according to need (in other words, no teleology built in here) – and in the struggle, some of these variations will prove of value to their possessors and so there will be an ongoing winnowing, what Darwin called "natural selection." This will lead to change, and the point is that this process points to the creation of design-like organic attributes. This was not a chance discovery. It was something that framed the whole discussion.

> How have all those exquisite adaptations of one part of the organisation to another part, and to the conditions of life, and of one distinct organic being to another being, been perfected? We see these beautiful co-adaptations most plainly in the woodpecker and missletoe; and only a little less plainly in the humblest parasite which clings to the hairs of a quadruped or feathers of a bird; in the structure of the beetle which dives through the water; in the plumed seed which is wafted by the gentlest breeze; in short, we see beautiful adaptations everywhere and in every part of the organic world. (61)

The answer is natural selection and with this we have a solution to the nature of organisms as legitimate as any in science. It is not that final causes are being denied. It is that they are being explained in terms of efficient causes.

> When we no longer look at an organic being as a savage looks at a ship, as at something wholly beyond his comprehension; when we regard every production of nature as one which has had a history; when we contemplate every complex structure and instinct as the summing up of many contrivances, each useful to the possessor, nearly in the same way as when we look at any great mechanical invention as the summing up of the labour, the experience, the

reason, and even the blunders of numerous workmen; when we thus view each organic being, how far more interesting, I speak from experience, will the study of natural history become! (485)

God?

At once people saw what was going on. This may have been basic science, but it was science with nasty implications for God-belief. Until then, we had what philosophers call an "inference to the best explanation." Something had to explain adaptation/contrivance. Blind law does not do so. Ergo, God is the best explanation. Now, Darwin was saying that blind law can do the job. So the God explanation is less compelling. Adam Sedgwick, a professor of geology at the University of Cambridge, and an old friend and mentor of Darwin – not without a sense of humor, for he referred to himself as a "son of a monkey" – saw this full well. "I call (in the abstract) causation the will of God: & I can prove that He acts for the good of His creatures. He also acts by laws which we can study & comprehend – Acting by law, & under what is called final cause, comprehends, I think, your whole principle." Except of course the principle doesn't do the job. "I humbly accept God's revelation of himself both in His works & in His word; & do my best to act in conformity with that knowledge which He only can give me, & He only can sustain me in doing" (Darwin 1985, 7: Letter from Sedgwick to Darwin, November 24, 1859).

We will discuss in some detail the exact implications of Darwin's theory for the theism-atheism debate. But we can say this straight off. Richard Dawkins (1986) was right when he said that after Darwin, it was finally possible to be "an intellectually fulfilled" atheist. The stranglehold of the design argument was, if not broken, then at least loosened. And now, perhaps not surprisingly, we do start to see a growing number of nonbelievers making their positions known. Darwin was raised a Christian, a member of the Church of England (Anglican or Episcopalian), probably given his family's detestation of slavery at the evangelical end of things. At Cambridge, he intended to be a clergyman. This avocation faded on the *Beagle* voyage, and his thinking moved from theism to deism. He held to this right through *Origin*. "Authors of the highest eminence seem to be fully satisfied with the view that each species has been independently created. To my mind it accords better with what we know of the laws impressed on matter by the Creator, that the production and extinction of the past and present inhabitants of the world should have been due to secondary causes, like those determining the birth and death of the individual" (488). Despite the fact that Darwin constantly toyed with the text, right through the six editions until 1872, this passage went unchanged, although it is true that, by then, Darwin's beliefs had faded. Never atheism. He would have thought that almost vulgar and associated with disgusting practices like birth control. To a correspondent (John Fordyce) in 1879, Darwin wrote: "In my most extreme fluctuations I have never been an atheist in the sense of denying the existence of a God. – I think that generally (& more and more so as I grow older) but not always, that an agnostic would be the most correct description of my state of mind" (Letter 12041, Darwin Correspondence Project).

What is interesting about Darwin is that he reflected almost all mid-Victorian intellectuals in that it was not science as such that pushed him toward nonbelief. It was the problems inherent in religion – Christianity – itself that made for the repudiation of childhood beliefs. For Darwin, totally unacceptable was the Pauline claim that nonbelief would lead to hellfire and damnation. "Knowing that a man is not justified by the works of the law, but by the faith of Jesus Christ, even we have believed in Jesus Christ, that we might be justified by the faith of Christ, and not by the works of the law: for by the works of the law shall no flesh be justified" (Galatians 2:16). Darwin's beloved father and older brother were both nonbelievers. He could not accept that they were thereby condemned.

> I can indeed hardly see how anyone ought to wish Christianity to be true; for if so the plain language of the text seems to show that the men who do not believe, and this would include my Father, Brother and almost all my best friends, will be everlastingly punished.
>   And this is a damnable doctrine. (Darwin 1958, 87)

What, then, was the chief effect of *Origin* on people's religious beliefs? It made nonbelief possible if one had other reasons for nonbelief. As important, notions like the struggle for existence made the very idea of a caring God seem difficult or absent. One could of course turn to the God of Job, who at times seems almost capricious in his attitude toward human beings, but generally people wanted a loving, caring God – the father of the parable of the prodigal son. Now He seemed to be gone. Poet and novelist Thomas Hardy was raised a good Anglican. Yet, by the middle of the decade after *Origin*, he had turned from his childhood beliefs.

> If but some vengeful god would call to me
> From up the sky, and laugh: "Thou suffering thing,
> Know that thy sorrow is my ecstasy,
> That thy love's loss is my hate's profiting!"
>
> Then would I bear it, clench myself, and die,
> Steeled by the sense of ire unmerited;
> Half-eased in that a Powerfuller than I
> Had willed and meted me the tears I shed.

> But not so. How arrives it joy lies slain,
> And why unblooms the best hope ever sown?
> —Crass Casualty obstructs the sun and rain,
> And dicing Time for gladness casts a moan . . .
> These purblind Doomsters had as readily strown
> Blisses about my pilgrimage as pain.
>
> (Hardy 1994, 5)

God just doesn't care.

Into the Twentieth Century

Let us bring the story up to date. Most intellectuals were like agnostic like Darwin. There were some atheists, most notably in Britain free thinker Charles Bradlaugh, who battled for several years (ultimately successfully) to get admitted to Parliament without having to take a religious oath. In America, Colonel (he had fought in the Civil War) Robert Ingersoll had a similar role. "The doctrine that future happiness depends upon belief is monstrous. It is the infamy of infamies. The notion that faith in Christ is to be rewarded by an eternity of bliss, while a dependence upon reason, observation and experience merits everlasting pain, is too absurd for refutation, and can be relieved only by that unhappy mixture of insanity and ignorance, called 'faith'" (1874). Coming into the twentieth century, we all know that there have been societies explicitly atheistic. Stalin's Russia for a start. Mao's China for a second. Karl Marx was their inspiration. "Religious suffering is, at one and the same time, the expression of real suffering and a protest against real suffering. Religion is the sigh of the oppressed creature, the heart of a heartless world, and the soul of soulless conditions. It is the opium of the people" (Marx 1844). In the Third Reich, where Marx had less hold – for a start, he was Jewish – there was certainly nonbelief. But not uniform, state-enforced atheism, as in Russia and China. Hitler was no Christian, but he believed strongly in a kind of divine-driven destiny. It was this that drove him in 1941 to make the disastrous attack on the Soviet Union.

Probably the most famous Anglophone atheist of the twentieth century was philosopher (and aristocrat) Bertrand Russell (1927). Many of his arguments were familiar. Equally familiar was the moral tone of his anti-God arguments. Again and again, he stressed how Christian practices led to horrendously wrong behavior, for instance, forcing people (usually women) into and keeping up marriages that were abusive in every sense of the word. It is true that Russell tended to speak to a restricted audience – for instance, to the listeners of the BBC's Radio Three, a kind of high-powered version of NPR. But he was in tune with a general attitude and movement in the middle of the century. More and more people simply found that the message of Christianity is irrelevant and in the way of genuine progress. Church attendance in countries like Britain and Canada dropped dramatically. In the Dominion (to use the technically proper name for countries in the British Commonwealth), attendance declined from 65 percent after the war to around 13 percent in this past decade. It was less that people became atheist or even agnostic. It was more that, like for my Canadian-born wife, religion – Christianity – was simply of no interest or compelling quality. A bit like the crinoline, it was something people did in years past. It didn't help the cause of faith that so much seemed irrelevant. A prime example was in the 1960s, when Pope Paul VI declared artificial contraception immoral – a decade when the pill gave women their own power over their sexuality.

The Exception

America, as so often, was and is different. The men behind the American Revolution tended to be deists. Benjamin Franklin was typical. However, as the years went by, it became more and more clear that so sophisticated a world picture hardly spoke to the psychological needs of the members of the new nation, often working in conditions of considerable hardship and danger. Something more robust was needed, and the evangelical preachers provided it (Porterfield 2012). The Second Great Awakening (the first was a century earlier, with the coming of religions like Methodism), in the 1830s, saw the rise of a home-grown, Bible-based Protestantism, tailor-made for the needs of the people. With the advent of cheap forms of mechanical printing, the Good Book could be made available to all (white people) who would find guides for life – parents to each other and to children, masters and mistresses to workers and employees, citizens to the state. Lack of formal education was no great barrier. Had not St. Paul said: "God hath chosen the foolish things of the world to confound the wise; and God hath chosen the weak things of the world to confound the things which are mighty" (1 Corinthians 1:27).

Inevitably, this got all caught up in the great slavery issue. As Northerners quoted the Bible to justify emancipation, so Southerners found comfort and support in the Bible for their position (Noll 2002). Although Sarah later turned against Hagar (when she had her own child), she had little compunction about offering Hagar to Abraham, or he in accepting the offer. St. Paul did not preach emancipation. True, he asked the master to treat his slave well, but he sent the slave back to the master. After the Civil War, if anything, the literalism of the South became even more extreme, with the analogy of the Israelites in captivity the theme of many a sermon. God chastises most those whom He loves most. And so it continued through the nineteenth century and into the twentieth. Note that, although this literalism was mainly a Southern-based phenomenon, it resonated with many people as the country expanded west. Also, with the lower-middle/upper-lower classes in the big cities of the North. They felt excluded by the successes of capitalism and threatened by the immigrants – Catholic and Jewish – from the countries of Europe.

It was almost inevitable that Darwin's theory of evolution got caught up in all of this (Numbers 2006). Historians have now shown definitively that it was not the science as such that was the great threat – paradoxically, today's literalists accept a great deal of evolution through natural selection at what they call the "micro level" – but the overall feeling that this was Northern thinking and ideology being imposed on the rest of the country. It didn't help that this sort of thing was often mixed up with sex education and the emancipation of women and that sort of thing. Most famously, this all came to a head in the mid-1920s, in the state of Tennessee, when a schoolteacher – John Thomas Scopes – was indicted for teaching evolution in a biology class (Larson 1997). Prosecuted by three-times presidential candidate William Bryan Jennings and defended by noted lawyer Clarence Darrow (fresh off defending Leopold and Loeb for the murder of Bobby Franks), the trial became a circus thanks in large part to the inflammatory reporting of *Baltimore Sun* journalist H. L. Menken. Although Scopes was found guilty, the verdict was later overturned on a technicality.

Creationism

This all had a chilling effect on the teaching of evolution, and mention of Darwin was removed from school biology texts – paradoxically at a time when the theory was making immense steps because of the synthesis of Darwinian selection with Mendelian genetics. Things were not to change until the late 1950s when, in response to the perceived Soviet superiority in science and technology thanks to *Sputnik*, American science education was radically updated and evolution was brought fully and openly into biology texts. To every action there is an equal and opposite reaction, and this led to a resurgence of evolution-denying biblical literalism. It was now given the name "Creationism," or "Scientific Creationism" since supposedly it was as good science as it was theology (and thus could rightfully be taught in state-supported public schools). The bible of the new movement, *Genesis Flood* (1961), was written by biblical scholar John C. Whitcomb and hydraulic engineer Henry M. Morris. It was the definitive statement of "Young Earth Creationism" – divine creation 6,000 years ago, six days in which all was accomplished, a universal flood wiping out all except a few chosen ones on a specially constructed ark, and the rest of the story. Interestingly, the book

reflected the times as much as did the new textbooks. As they were spurred by
the Cold War so was *Genesis Flood*. The emphasis on the Flood rather than
(say) the more obvious story of Adam and Eve and the Garden of Eden was
a function of the authors' dispensationalism – the belief that history comes in
spans marked at the end of each by an event of great significance. The Flood is
the second dispensation (after the expulsion from Eden) and anticipates the final
dispensation, the coming of Armageddon, surely started by a nuclear
conflagration.

In respects, this new Creationism caught the scientific community flatfooted,
a realization that came in 1981 when the state of Arkansas passed a bill
demanding, in state-funded biology classes, "balanced treatment" between
evolution and Creationism. Fortunately, the new law was ruled unconstitu-
tional – an improper blending of state and church – and that threat diminished
(Ruse 1988a), to be replaced hydra-like with a new version, Intelligent Design
Theory (IDT). Taking no stand on such things as the age of the universe, it
insisted nevertheless that the past can be understood only if one allowed a series
of divine interventions. The Christian God is not paraded too prominently, but
everyone understands that the Designer is not a grad student on Andromeda
using the Earth as a dissertation-writing experiment (Pennock 1998).

Although, like Creationism, IDT was defeated in the law courts and thus
unable officially to be taught in publicly funded schools, one suspects that –
thanks particularly to the growth of charter schools – today more Genesis is
taught to young Americans than at any point in the republic's history. Moreover,
as in the past, anti-evolutionism is more a flag for a general religiously based
attack on modernism – anti-women's rights, anti-contraception and antiabortion, antigay and anti-lesbian, against just about anything embraced by liberals
in the past 200 years. Phillip Johnson, the intellectual grandfather of the IDT
movement, is as obsessed about cross-dressing as he is about evolution. It turns
out, however, that cross-dressing has a specific meaning for Johnson. He does
not think the average liberal professor goes home at night and slips on a silk,
pink nightie. He is worried about stroppy broads (to use a not unheard description) in pantsuits having positions of authority. Nancy Pelosi comes at once to
mind. It is not what the Bible sanctions. "Let your women keep silence in the
churches: for it is not permitted unto them to speak; but they are commanded to
be under obedience, as also saith the law. And if they will learn any thing, let
them ask their husbands at home: for it is a shame for women to speak in the
church" (1 Corinthians 14:34–35).

Not only are young Americans being fed this sort of stuff. Like Coca-Cola,
biblical literalism is an all-American product that travels well. It has taken firm
root in many European countries. In a world that sees such lands embracing

eagerly the isolationism and authoritarianism of the 1930s, what would one expect? They are ripe for the propaganda of the American evangelical literalists. Ultra-orthodox Jews are ready listeners, as are conservative Muslims and others. For all that religious belief has fallen dramatically, particularly in secular societies of the West, it would be a bad mistake to think that this is the end of religion, especially religion of the more literalistic type. Such then is the background to the main actors of our next section.

2 The New Atheists

Why Now?

In the first decade of this new century, atheism suddenly exploded into view. Fiery tracts were written in its favor and equally fiery tracts were written against it. The champions of atheism – the so-called New Atheists – became media darlings. Predictably, the more the staid and respectable raged against them, the more their books scaled best-seller heights hitherto undreamed of. There are several reasons atheism suddenly became such a subject of interest, and it would be unfair and churlish to deny the force of argumentation of the leaders of the movement – Richard Dawkins, author of *Selfish Gene* and hugely famous science writer; Sam Harris, then a graduate student in neurobiology; Daniel Dennett, a philosopher well known for his embrace of a materialistic approach to the body-mind problem; and (now deceased) Christopher Hitchens, also well known as a journalist and scourge of the famous and self-satisfied, like Mother Teresa.

However, for all the talents of these writers – often semi-humorously referred to as the "Four Horsemen of the Apocalypse" – external factors played an as big or bigger role. Mention was made at the end of the previous section of the way in which American evangelicals especially promoted their beliefs, which they attempted (as they still do) to impose on all, believers or not. Anti-contraception, antiabortion, anti-feminism, anti-LGBTQ, anti-just-about-everything-else, except items like the promotion of Israel (the founding of which is taken to be a harbinger of the last judgment). Evangelicals are large in number, vocal in their demands, and politically very astute. They are not, however, the only members of society – not even a majority, if you take into account liberal Christians and Jews and those of other faiths, as well as nonbelievers. For many, there was reason to distrust and dislike religion, especially extreme forms of religion.

Evangelicals tend to be Protestant, although Catholics can equal them when it comes to such issues as abortion and gay rights and tolerance. Catholics, however, had their own reasons for others to distrust and dislike their religion.

Although some was known before, it was early in the decade that the *Boston Globe* reported on horrendous accounts of sexual abuse by Catholic clergy, much that was concealed or denied by the hierarchy. One learns that at least 5 percent of Catholic clergy are known sexual predators, with many years of abuse of the young, especially boys. No one could think this purely contingent. You take an idealistic boy of eighteen and confine him to a society where he is forbidden the natural instincts of humans for emotional intimacy and love and sexual activity. Is it any wonder that so many fall and behave in dreadful ways? Especially given the authority and status that priests are given over their congregations, particularly the young? The desires are there. The opportunities are there. And the people in charge work nonstop to cover up and maintain the status quo. All in the name of Jesus Christ.

Then to add to the stew a third element – the overwhelming and urgent element – came 9/11, when Muslim fanatics flew two aircraft into the New York City Twin Towers and another into the Pentagon in Washington. A fourth failed to cause great damage only because of the extreme bravery of the passengers who were able to divert the plane even though they could not save themselves. Although, starting with the president, there were pleas not to let this taint our views of Muslims, or of religious people generally, even the more tolerant felt that this was a vile reflection of aspects of religion. Almost paradoxically, those who were most intolerant in their own faiths were those who had the least understanding of the fanaticism of other faiths. It was pointless to argue that many other factors were involved, starting with the ways in which the West uses and appropriates the things of the East – people and oil most obviously – the damage was done. Religion is a bad thing.

With this as background, let us see what the New Atheists had to say. Given his preeminence, not to mention the runaway sales of his book, *The God Delusion*, as my template I take Dawkins's arguments, dividing them into sections. Expectedly, there is a certain sameness and overlap in the arguments of others, so, rather than give them independent treatment, as appropriate I introduce the claims of the other big three. Others wrote in similar mode, notably University of Chicago evolutionist Jerry Coyne, and again as appropriate I refer to them. I do not claim that the New Atheists were the only people then arguing for atheism, or for any kind of nonbelief – I myself was known for having publicly forsworn the Christianity of my childhood. As a contrast, waiting (somewhat atypically) to the end of this Element to introduce my own take on things, I here refer to the thinking of today's most eminent evolutionary biologist, Edward O. Wilson of Harvard. He is as firm in his atheism as Richard Dawkins, but his thinking goes in somewhat different ways. As far as possible, at this stage I present the arguments in a disinterested fashion, trying not to slip in judgments, implicit or explicit. The reader is warned that one of the objects of scorn in *The God Delusion* is one Michael Ruse. I guess I am included in the general contempt for philosophers, but I am privileged by my own special mention. In my efforts to bring science and religion into some form of harmony, I am likened to the pusillanimous appeaser of Munich, Neville Chamberlain. We are also told that perhaps there should be "a First Rule of Science Journalism." Namely: "Interview at least one person other than Michael Ruse" (Dawkins 2006, 68 n). I leave to others who know my personality better than I to judge whether these comments leave me dispirited and downcast or rather cheery and chuffed.[1]

Which Religion?

Appropriately for the series in which this Element is placed, *The God Delusion* is focused exclusively on monotheism, meaning the three great faiths in the Abrahamic tradition – Judaism, Christianity, and Islam. Not that Dawkins sees much difference between them. "For most of my purposes, all three Abrahamic religions can be treated as indistinguishable." He adds, "I shall have Christianity mostly in mind." This is a function of familiarity, although for "my purposes the differences matter less than the similarities." Eastern religions such as Buddhism and Confucianism are ignored. "Indeed, there is something to be said for treating these not as religions at all but as ethical systems or philosophies of life" (2006, 37–38).

Interestingly, Sam Harris would probably be comfortable with this conclusion. He agrees that in *The End of Faith* (2004), he has "not said much that is derogatory of Buddhism," adding: "This is not an accident. While Buddhism has also been a source of ignorance and occasional violence, it is not a religion of faith, or a religion at all, in the Western sense" (283). Lest that sound a little begrudging, he goes on to say that "it remains true that the esoteric teachings of Buddhism offer the most complete methodology we have for discovering the intrinsic freedom of consciousness, unencumbered by any dogma."

Eastern religions to one side, other New Atheists focus more or less exclusively on the Abrahamic religions. With 9/11 so vividly before him, Harris spends considerable time discussing Islam. Generally, however, the focus is on Christianity in particular. Dennett, in his *Breaking the Spell* (2006), goes so far as to make a virtue of his blinkered vision. He tells us: "I am an American author and this book is addressed in the first place to American readers" (xiii). Because of the limitations of his knowledge, "my focus on Christianity first, and Islam

---

[1] In *The God Delusion*, Dawkins tells us that he likes to use English slang to stretch the linguistic horizons of Americans. I follow in the steps of the master.

and Judaism next, is unintended but unavoidable." He just doesn't know that much about other religions. You might fault him for not doing his homework, "but since the urgency of the message was borne in on me again and again by current events, I had to settle for the perspectives I had managed to achieve so far" (xiv).

Coming from a somewhat different perspective, Edward O. Wilson, a child of the American South and raised a Southern Baptist, tends to see all religion through the lens of his early years. Even Buddhism sounds like something from the world of revivals and camp meetings. Let us have no nonsense about pacifism. For all the talk about loving and helping others, Buddhism settles into familiar patterns when the chips are down. In Wilson's Pulitzer Prize–winning *On Human Nature* (1978), we learn that: "While embracing the concept of universal compassion, both Buddhist and Christian countries have found it expedient to wage aggressive wars, many of which they justify in the name of religion" (154–155). The end, too, all sounds pretty familiar. "A few Burmese Buddhists, it may be noted, work ultimately towards nirvana as a form of extinction, but most conceive of it as a kind of permanent paradise" (244).

Hatred of Religion

As one might say that the essence of a right-angled triangle is that one of the corners is 90°, so one might say that the essence of New Atheism writing is a hatred of religion. Dawkins sets the tone. "The oldest of the three Abrahamic religions, and the clear ancestor of the other two, is Judaism: originally a tribal cult of a single fiercely unpleasant God, morbidly obsessed with sexual restrictions, with the smell of charred flesh, with his own superiority over rival gods and with the exclusiveness of his chosen desert tribe" (Dawkins 2006, 35). Harris suspects mental disorder. "It takes a certain kind of person to believe what no one else believes. To be ruled by ideas for which you have no evidence (and which therefore cannot be justified in conversation with other human beings) is generally a sign that something is seriously wrong with your mind. Clearly, there is sanity in numbers" (2004, 72).

In *God Is Not Great* (2007), Christopher Hitchens's rhetoric does credit to tabloid journalism. He tells us that he is happy to go to the bar mitzvahs of the children of religious friends, to admire their Gothic cathedrals, and not to quibble at the idea that the Koran was dictated in Arabic to an illiterate merchant. "And as it happens, I will continue to do this without insisting on the polite reciprocal condition – which is *that they in turn leave me alone*. But this, religion is ultimately incapable of doing. As I write these words, and as you read them, people of faith are in their different ways planning your and my destruction, and the destruction of all the hard-won human attainments that I have touched upon. *Religion poisons everything*" (13).

Daniel Dennett goes Darwinian. He thinks religion is a parasite, a virus on humans, just as much as the liver fluke is a parasite on sheep. "You watch an ant in a meadow, laboriously climbing up a blade of grass, higher and higher until it falls, then climbs again, and again, like Sisyphus rolling his rock, always striving to reach the top." Why does this happen? The ant gets nothing out of all this activity. "Its brain has been commandeered by a tiny parasite, a lancet fluke (*Dicrocelium dendriticum*), that needs to get itself into the stomach of a sheep or cattle in order to complete its reproductive cycle. This little brain worm is driving the ant into position to benefit *its* progeny, not the ant's" (2006, 3–4). Just as the liver fluke is up to no good for sheep, so religion is up to no good for humans.

To be fair, Dennett, unlike the others, does see that religion can have the potential for good. "Religion provides some people with a motivated organization for doing great things – working for social justice, education, political action, economic reform, and so forth." Unfortunately, for some people, aspects of religion "are more toxic, exploiting less savory aspects of their psychology, playing on guilt, loneliness, the longing for self-esteem and importance" (310). Without wanting to get too psychoanalytic about what drives a fellow philosopher, in trying to be balanced I sense here the motivation of a university professor rather than (as with other New Atheists) that of a polemicist pure and simple – well, simple at least.

Wilson again is somewhat of an anomaly. One certainly does not get the outright hatred of the New Atheists. If anything, there is a kind of melancholic, loving memory of a childhood sweetheart. In *The Creation* (2006), he writes to an imaginary Baptist minister about the grave ecological crises facing us all. But he does not do so with scorn and mistrust. He can no longer accept the minister's beliefs, but he thinks there is common ground, enough for them to solve the crises together. Wilson begins his letter by telling the story of Charles Darwin and of his trip on the *Beagle* that brought him to the rainforests of Brazil. "It is not possible to give an adequate understanding of the higher feelings of wonder, admiration, and devotion which fill and elevate the mind" (7). Then at the end: "I hope you will not have taken offence when I spoke of ascending to Nature instead of ascending away from it. It would give me deep satisfaction to find that expression as I have explained it compatible with your own beliefs" (168).

Religion a Scientific Question

This is a shared theme. Dawkins takes without argument that the God question is a scientific question. "Either he exists or he doesn't. It is a scientific question;

one day we may know the answer, and meanwhile we can say something pretty strong about the probability" (2006, 48). In the end, it all comes down to naked mud wrestling: God versus Darwin. Dawkins characterizes the "God Hypothesis" thus: "*there exists a super-human, supernatural intelligence who deliberately designed and created the universe and everything in it, including us.*" Dawkins's alternative: "*any creative intelligence of sufficient complexity to design anything, comes into existence only as the end product of an extended process of gradual evolution.*" Dawkins's conclusion? "God, in the sense defined, is an illusion . . . a pernicious delusion" (31).

Harris thinks much the same way. It is true that "intellectuals as diverse as H. G. Wells, Albert Einstein, Carl Jung, Max Plank, Freeman Dyson, and Stephen Jay Gould have declared the war between reason and faith to be long over. On this view, there is no need to have all our beliefs about the universe cohere. A person can be a God-fearing Christian on Sunday and a working scientist come Monday morning, without ever having to account for the partition that seems to have erected itself in his head while he slept." But this is all a fairy tale, brought on by the tolerant kind of society in which we live. Other societies see full well the incompatibility of science and religion, meaning that science shows religion to be false and untenable. "In places where scholars can still be stoned to death for doubting the veracity of the Koran, Gould's notion of a 'loving concordat' between faith and reason would be perfectly delusional" (2004, 16).

In *Faith versus Fact* (2015), the Jiminy Cricket of the New Atheist movement, Jerry Coyne, speaks of Charles Darwin's *Origin of Species* as the "greatest scripture-killer ever penned," arguing that "science and religion are engaged in a kind of war: a war for understanding, a war about whether we should have good reasons for what we accept as true" (xii). Like all true believers, Coyne has a statement of faith.

> My claim is this: science and religion are incompatible because they have different methods for getting knowledge about reality, have different ways of assessing the reliability of that knowledge, and, in the end, arrive at conflicting conclusions about the universe. "Knowledge" acquired by religion is at odds not only with scientific knowledge, but also with knowledge professed by other religions. In the end, religion's methods, unlike those of science, are useless for understanding reality. (64)

Again, Wilson is a contrast. Of course, he sees claims about Genesis-based miraculous creations as incompatible with science, with evolutionary biology. But with no hatred of religion and with a firm belief that religious belief is genetically engrained in the human psyche and hence will never be eliminated, he is inclined to see religion less as at war with science and more as being taking over by it. In the language of philosophers, it is less one of Kuhnian paradigms and more one of the reduction of one (earlier) theory to a (later) more powerful theory. It is less one of phlogiston and oxygen and more one of Newton and Einstein. "But make no mistake about the power of scientific materialism. It presents the human mind with an alternative mythology that until now has always, point for point in zones of conflict, defeated traditional religion." We must now have a kind of secular religion, based on evolution. "Its narrative form is the epic: the evolution of the universe from the big bang of fifteen years ago through the origin of the elements and celestial bodies to the beginnings of life on earth" (Wilson 1978, 192). He concludes: "Theology is not likely to survive as an independent intellectual discipline." It goes without saying that this is reduction with a bite. Wilson is not about to show that "God exists" follows from the premises of Darwinian evolutionary biology. Rather the belief that "God exists" follows from the premises of Darwinian evolutionary biology, together, no doubt, with a great deal of empirical spadework.

God's Existence

The God Delusion takes us through the classic proofs for the existence of God. First up is the ontological argument. Originating with Anselm, it is the paradigm of simplicity. God is the greatest thing that could be conceived. Does God, thus defined, exist? If He does not exist, then there is a greater, namely a God who is existing. This is a reductio and so necessarily God must exist. Dawkins does not so much analyze the moves and show the fallacy as dismiss it with a sneer, referring to it as "an infantile argument" (2006, 80). He adds: "I mean it as a compliment when I say that you could almost define a philosopher as someone who won't take common sense for an answer" (83). With friends like this, who needs enemies?

The causal argument – everything has a cause, the world is a thing, therefore the world had a cause: God! – gets more treatment. The classic response comes as a question: What caused God? This is essentially Dawkins's response, couched in terms of complexity. He is much struck by the complex nature of the universe and refuses to accept that God, who traditionally is defined as something ontologically simple, could do the job. God hypotheses raise "bigger problems than they solve. How do they cope with the argument that any God capable of designing a universe, carefully and thoughtfully tuned to our evolu-tion must be a supremely complex and improbable entity who needs an even bigger explanation than the one he is supposed to provide?" (147). He adds that "a God capable of designing a universe would have to be complex and

statistically improbable" (153). Unfortunately, "the designer hypothesis imme-
diately raises the larger problem of who designed the designer. The whole
problem we started out with was the problem of explaining statistical improb-
ability. It is obviously no solution to postulate something even more improbable" (158).

You cannot get complexity out of simplicity. But you can out of Darwin.
Complexity, certainly functioning complexity, spells design. It could not have
happened by chance. Ergo, the third big argument for God's existence.
Complexity spells design; design spells God. Not so. "Darwinian evolution,
specifically natural selection, ... shatters the illusion of design within the
domain of biology, and teaches us to be suspicious of any kind of design
hypothesis in physics and cosmology as well." (Dawkins is referring here to
attempts to find design in the close-fitting nature of the basic constants of the
universe – close fitting in a way that allows for the evolution of humankind. The
so-called Anthropic Principle.)

Not much more to be said after this. Interestingly, the one who might have
been expected to contribute most to the discussion, philosopher Dan Dennett, is
almost reticent on the subject. I think much is to do with the point hinted at
earlier, that he is more interested in seeing why religion captivates rather than
just why religion is wrong – which he basically takes as his starting point.
Perhaps this is linked to a constitutional inability to take natural theology
seriously, something that is clearly an important part of Dawkins's psyche.
About the move by defenders of the causal (cosmological) argument that God
is in some sense self-caused, and hence necessary, Dennett is more impatient
than thoughtfully insightful.

> What caused God? The reply that God is self-caused (somehow) then raises
> the rebuttal: If something can be self-caused, why can't the universe as
> a whole be the thing that is self-caused? This leads in various arcane direc-
> tions, in the strange precincts of string theory and probability functions and
> the like, at one extreme, and into ingenious nitpicking about the meaning of
> "cause" at the other. Unless you have a taste for mathematics and theoretical
> physics on the one hand, or the niceties of scholastic logic on the other, you
> are not apt to find any of this compelling, or even fathomable. (2006, 243)

End of discussion! Truly, for Wilson has little to say about God's existence,
simply assuming that He is not real and is rather a function of human imagina-
tion. Wilson is more interested in why we imagine the kind of God that He
supposedly is. "The God of monotheistic religions is always male; this strong
patriarchal tendency has several cultural sources. Pastoral societies are highly
mobile, tightly organized, and often militant, all features that tip the balance
toward male authority" (1978, 190). Note that the key occupation is herding of

stock, another exclusively male role, and a reason Judaism (and continuing to the other religions) speaks of God as a shepherd and of us as His lambs.

Faith

Perhaps the problem is that we are going at the problem of religion in the wrong way. We have been stressing reason. That is what natural theology is all about. Perhaps we should have been stressing faith, revealed theology. It is interesting and probably telling that this is not a major concern of Wilson. He recognizes faith, clearly thinks it wrong or inadequate, but is less into scolding it (or its devotees) and more into explaining it in biological terms. Reduction. The New Atheists take a very different approach. The big guns really do come into play. Faith is something that comes to you without external evidence or reasoning, even of the crudest kind. And therein lies the problem. "Faith is an evil precisely because it requires no justification and brooks no argument" (Dawkins 2006, 308). Expectedly, given the title of his book, it is Sam Harris who really makes a meal out of the faith question. Dismissing people like Paul Tillich who try to take a more sophisticated view of faith, Harris states flatly that "the truth is that religious faith is simply unjustified belief in matters of ultimate concern – specifically in propositions that promise some mechanism by which human life can be spared the ravages of time and death. Faith is what credulity becomes when it finally achieves escape velocity from the constraints of terrestrial discourse – constraints like reasonableness, internal coherence, civility, and candor" (2004, 65).

Christianity is bad enough. "Auschwitz, the Cathar heresy, the witch hunts – these phrases signify depths of human depravity and human suffering that would surely elude description were a writer to set himself no other task" (106). This is nothing to Islam. It may indeed be our moral duty to kill such faith-driven fanatics. "The link between belief and behavior raises the stakes considerably. Some propositions are so dangerous that it may even be ethical to kill people for believing them." Harsh, but necessary. "Certain beliefs place their adherents beyond the reach of every peaceful means of persuasion, while inspiring them to commit acts of extraordinary violence against others" (52–53).

Jerry Coyne (2015) mops up. The problem is not with religion as such but in "its reliance on and glorification of faith – belief, or if you will, 'trust' or 'confidence' – without supporting evidence." Faith is dangerous both to science and to society. "The danger to science is how faith warps the public under-standing of science: by arguing, for instance, that science is based just as strongly on faith as is religion; by claiming that revelation or the guidance of ancient books is just as reliable a guide to the truth about our universe, as are the tools of science; by thinking that an adequate explanation can be based on what is personally appealing rather than what stands the test of empirical study" (225–226). Society? Well, this leads to issues we discuss shortly, especially children.

Why Religion?

In the face of something so obviously false, why do we have and support religions? As one firmly committed to the Darwinian nature of culture – in *The Selfish Gene*, he introduced the idea of "memes," cultural units akin to the biological units of genes – Dawkins floats several explanations, all ultimately based on the nonadaptive utility of religion itself and hence in some sense perverting the evolutionary process. One that he quite favors is that religion is a by-product of something with real adaptive value. This by-product, he suggests, might stem from the clear biological utility of learning from your seniors, your parents, and others. Stay away from the cliff. Red berries give you stomachache. Crocodiles are not friendly.

Karl Popper says that we learn from our mistakes, but some mistakes are better not made in the first place. "To say the least, there will be a selective advantage to child brains that possess the rule of thumb: believe, without question, whatever your grown-ups tell you. Obey your parents, obey the tribal elders, especially when they adopt a solemn, minatory tone. Trust your elders without question" (Dawkins 2006, 174). Regrettably, they are not always right and can lead you astray. Religious belief could be a prime example. As one who, like Dawkins, was incarcerated in tender years in an English public (private, prep) school, one hears the voice of one's late headmaster laying down the law on matters essential, from the vulgarity of the used-car-salesman practice of wearing suede shoes to the ophthalmological dangers of self-abuse.

Dennett (2006) is a faithful follower of the memes hypothesis. The story about parasites and religion is couched explicitly in terms of memes. Parasites are passing on their genes. Religions are passing on their memes. Religions are doing this for their good, not ours, and any benefits are entirely incidental. He argues that "the ultimate beneficiaries of religious adaptations are the memes themselves," although this does not preclude our being rational once conquered. However, "the initial capture need not be – indeed, should not be – a rational choice by the host" (186). Cleverly, Dennett cites William James for support. "One may say that the whole development of Christianity in inwardness has consisted in little more than the great and greater emphasis attached to this crisis of self-surrender" (186). One is reminded in this context of C. S. Lewis and his reluctant conversion to Christianity.

> You must picture me alone in that room in Magdalen, night after night, feeling, whenever my mind lifted even for a second from my work, the steady, unrelenting approach of Him whom I so earnestly desired not to meet. That which I greatly feared had at last come upon me. In the Trinity Term of 1929 I gave in, and admitted that God was God, and knelt and prayed: perhaps, that night, the most dejected and reluctant convert in all England. (Lewis 1955, 115)

Wilson does not use the language of memes, although he was to introduce a similar notion of "culturgen" (Ruse 1986). Really, though, he thinks such language is a bit superfluous, mainly probably because, although he acknowledges the role of culture, his heart is always in biology and the genes. Religion is a matter of natural selection and that mainly at the level of evolutionarily shaped biological heredity. "The genes hold culture on a leash" (Wilson 1978, 167). But why religion? "The highest forms of religious practice, when examined more closely, can be seen to confer biological advantage. Above all they congeal identity. In the midst of the chaotic and potentially disorienting experiences each person undergoes daily, religion classifies him, provides him with unquestioned membership in a group claiming great powers, and by this means gives him a driving purpose in life compatible with his self-interest. His strength is the strength of the group, his guide the sacred covenant" (188). Religion is an adaptation for group identity. No amount of reasoned argument is going to make religion go away. Wilson accepts the possibility – nay, the actuality – of secular religions like Marxism, but religion as such is fixed in the genes and only genetic manipulation could make a real difference.

Ethics

We must break the pattern. It is Edward O. Wilson who must open this section. It is he who sparked the whole, now-thriving discussion of nonreligious, evolutionary approaches to morality. For 100 years after Darwin published the *Descent of Man* (1871), "evolutionary ethics" was greeted with all the enthusiasm of a bad smell at a vicarage garden party. Anyone who thought that natural selection was relevant was either flaky or promoting some vile libertarian view of human nature. Then came Wilson with a philosophical sledgehammer.

> Camus said that the only serious philosophical question is suicide. That is wrong even in the strict sense intended. A biologist, who is concerned with questions of physiology and evolutionary history, realizes that self-

knowledge is constrained and shaped by the emotional control centers in the
hypothalamus and limbic system of the brain. These centers flood our consciousness with all the emotions – hate, love, guilt, fear, and others – that are
consulted by ethical philosophers who wish to intuit the standards of good
and evil. What, we are then compelled to ask, made the hypothalamus and
limbic system? They evolved by natural selection. That simple biological
statement must be pursued to explain ethics and ethical philosophers, if not
epistemology and epistemologists, at all depths. (1975, 3)

Like Darwin, Wilson thinks that selection shows that helping others can be
a good adaptive strategy, and (unlike Darwin) he thinks that this is all the
justification one could need. (Darwin was simply not interested in these kinds
of questions of justification. He thought of himself as a scientist, pure and
simple.) Let me give in full the quotation about genes and leashes.

The genes hold culture on a leash. The leash is very long, but inevitably
values will be constrained in accordance with their effects on the human gene
pool. The brain is a product of evolution. Human behavior – like the deepest
capacities for emotional response which drive and guide it – is the circuitous
technique by which human genetic material has been and will be kept intact.
Morality has no other demonstrable ultimate function. (1978, 167)

What then of the New Atheists? If religion is such a load of dangerous
nonsense, whence morality? It cannot be God's will, and psychological experi-
ments show that being religious doesn't really make you more moral. As for
Wilson, Darwinian evolution gives the answer, although for the New Atheists, it
is more one of substitution and opposition, than as, for Wilson, more one of
providing better support for what religion claims. In Dawkins's opinion, there
are "four good Darwinian reasons for individuals to be altruistic, generous or
'moral' towards each other" (2006, 219). First, there is aiding sharers of one's
genetic composition – relatives. Kin selection. Second, there is the "you scratch
my back, I'll scratch yours" principle. Reciprocal altruism. Third, there is "the
Darwinian benefit of acquiring a reputation for generosity and kindness."
Fourth, possibly, there is "the particular additional benefit of conspicuous
generosity as a way of buying unfakably authentic advertising."

Science gives the answers, although one gets the impression that more
important to Dawkins than making the positive case for Darwin is making the
negative case for religion. For all that, to be honest, "much of the Bible is not
systematically evil but just plain weird" (237), Dawkins has a grand time
parading a list of grotesque behaviors or practices supposedly mandated and
endorsed by God Almighty. Starting with the Old Testament, "the moral of the
story of Noah is appalling." God was cheesed off with the way things were
going, so, except for Noah and his pals on the Ark, He drowned the lot –

innocent as well as guilty. That is virtually the high point. The sordid behavior of Abraham is detailed in full. The story of Moses and the Midianites is no better. "But all the women children, that have not known a man by lying with him, keep alive for yourselves" (Numbers 31:18).

You might think the New Testament an improvement. Not really so. It is the case that Jesus comes off better, but note that this is often because he flouts the dictates of the Old Testament, for instance in arguing that the Sabbath was made for man, not man for the Sabbath. Even so, Jesus was a bit dodgy on family relationships and obligations, and St. Paul was appalling when it came to claims about original sin, namely that we are all guilty because of the sin of Adam, which could only be expunged by the death of Jesus on the cross. Substitutionary atonement. "What kind of ethical philosophy is it that condemns every child, even before it is born, to inherit the sin of a remote ancestor?" (251). Followed by a good dollop of sadomasochism. "God incarnated himself as a man, Jesus, in order that he should be tortured and executed in *atonement* for the hereditary sin of Adam" (252).

Moving briskly along, Dawkins deals with such issues as the atheism of Stalin and Hitler. Hitler is always cited as the paradigmatic example of an atheist putting his vile beliefs into action. "The truth of the matter is far from clear" (273). If his anti-Semitism did not come from Martin Luther, then it came directly from scripture. "But when he saw many of the Pharisees and Sadducees come to his baptism, he said unto them, O generation of vipers, who hath warned you to flee from the wrath to come?" (Matthew 3:7). The echo here is of a speech by Hitler when he referred to the Jews as "the brood of vipers and adders," adding "how terrific was His fight for the world against the Jewish poison." Also, there is the question of how we change our moral thinking – yesterday, slavery, today, all equal. The Zeitgeist (spirit of the times) changes. Both Thomas Henry Huxley and Abraham Lincoln accepted the intellectual inferiority of the negro. Today, we blush for them – as they would for themselves. Many factors probably account for the change, increased knowledge about humankind, for example. What you can safely bet is that it was not religion, which always lags behind. We do not "need God in order to be good, or to decide what is good" (Dawkins 2006, 272).

Other New Atheists back Dawkins to the hilt on the unimportance of religion for morality. Jerry Coyne (2015) argues that other species show rudiments of morality. There are good evolutionary reasons for this, leading to the conclusion that we have no need of the God hypothesis – "unless you think that God also installed morality in rats, monkeys, dogs, and crows" (172). Of the need for a God to support and justify morality, Dennett (2006) says: "There are two well-known problems with this reasoning: (1) it doesn't seem to be true, which is good news, since (2) it is such a demeaning view of human nature" (279). Like Dennett, most push the argument that religion only condones or increases immorality. Christopher Hitchens (2007) has little time for the Old Testament and even less for the New. One of his chapters has the title "The 'New' Testament Exceeds the Evil of the 'Old' One." Of a great moral leader like Martin Luther King, he writes that when he took a stand against racism, he "did so as a profound humanist and nobody could ever use his name to justify oppression or cruelty. He endures for that reason and his legacy has very little to do with his professed theology" (180). Not that Hitchens has much time for Eastern religions either. "A faith that despises the mind and the free individual, that preaches submission and resignation, and that regards life as a poor and transient thing, is ill-equipped for self criticism." Those who seek "enlightenment" in such directions "may think they are leaving the realm of despised materialism, but they are still being asked to put their reason to sleep, and to discard their minds along with their sandals" (204).

Children

And so, nigh seamlessly, to children, and to the immorality of indoctrinating them with religion. Expectedly, this is not a major issue for Wilson, who has a different take on religion from the New Atheists. He is more interested in reasons why people are interested in children at all. (Clue: Human beings are animals and, in the Darwinian world, reproduction is the name of the game. For sophisticated organisms like humans, reproduction demands lots of childcare by both sexes.) Here, however, as elsewhere, Wilson is an outlier. Richard Dawkins's passion, if anything, increases. Of all that he finds objectionable about religion it is the treatment and indoctrination of children. Asked in Dublin for his views on the sexual abuses of Catholic priests, he replied: "Horrible as sexual abuse no doubt was, the damage was arguably less than the long-term psychological damage inflicted by bringing the child up Catholic in the first place" (Dawkins 2006, 217). One might say that as horrifying for his critics is the fact that often Dawkins seems to downplay the nature and effects of priestly child sexual abuse. He was fondled himself as a child by a schoolmaster, but dismisses it as something that happened. He is keen not to judge yesterday by the standards of today. In *The God Delusion*, of those seeking monetary recompense for sexual sins long ago, he writes: "There's gold in them thar long-gone fumbles in the vestry" (317), adding that the supposed perpetrator is often dead and unable to defend himself. It is the indoctrination that draws Dawkins's real scorn and, to that end, he is prepared to minimize the rest.

Others share Dawkins's horrors of religious indoctrination. Christopher Hitchens writes: "We have no way to quantify the damage done by telling tens of millions of children that masturbation will make them blind, or that impure thoughts will lead to an eternity of torment, or that family members of other faiths including members of their own families will burn, or that venereal disease will result from kissing. Nor can we hope to quantify the damage done by holy instructors who rammed home these lies and accompanied them with floggings and rapes and public humiliations" (2007, 55–56). Others focus more on the effects. Jerry Coyne is eloquent on the sufferings of children because, on religious grounds, their parents refuse medical intervention and care. He tells the horrific story of Ashley King, who died in agony from a tumor on her leg – a tumor "about the size of two watermelons." Her parents fought, right down the line, to prevent regular practitioners from aiming to cure or at least to alleviate pain. They were Christian Scientists. Apparently, seventy-one Christian Scientist practitioners were praying for her well-being.

> Such deaths are unconscionable because they involve children who have no say – or no mature say – in their own medical care, but are at the mercy of their parents' beliefs. Because injuring a child by withholding medical care for nonreligious reasons constitutes legal child abuse, it's hard to make the case that it's not equally abusive when medical care is rejected on religious grounds." (Coyne 2015, 234)

Not much more to be said, and with this we can end our exposition of the New Atheists (and Wilson) on religion. Let us turn now to critical analysis, following the order of presentation in this section.

3 Critique

Why Now?

The New Atheists wrote with passion, above all against the background of 9/11 and the Muslim fanaticism that drove young men to hijack four airplanes in order to inflict great damage on the United States of America. Inevitably, after nearly twenty years without a comparable attack, tempers have cooled and emotions have subsided. There is, already, a somewhat stale air to much that they wrote. The sell-by date was soon reached, thanks in no small part to the immediate responses of believers. Alister and Joanna McGrath's *The Dawkins Delusion? Atheist Fundamentalism and the Denial of the Divine* (2007) and John Haught's *God and the New Atheism: A Critical Response to Dawkins, Harris, and Hitchens* (2008) are good examples of the genre. I was in the fight. I blurbed the McGrath book as showing how *The God Delusion* "made me ashamed to be an atheist." More seriously, turning to the New Atheists themselves, polemically it might be a good strategy to tear into the God of the Old Testament with the ferocity and scorn found in *The God Delusion*, but it is one-sided and transitory – as polemics usually are. Take the story of David and Bathsheba. God loved David, He really did. But when David transgressed, sending Bathsheba's husband to certain death, God was not pleased. He sent a prophet to see that David realize the wrong he had done and, as punishment, killed off the first child from the union of David and Bathsheba. This is not the deity introduced by Richard Dawkins: "a petty, unjust, unforgiving control-freak." Many nonbelievers know this. It does not turn them from their nonbelief, but it does point to inadequacies in the New Atheist onslaught.

Already there are more nuanced and subtle discussions of and defenses of atheism particularly and nonbelief more generally. To take but one example, the contributors to a handbook to atheism that I worked on a year or two back, having a young Christian as coeditor, showed fully how atheism takes on different meanings and nuances dependent on the situation in time and space (Bullivant and Ruse 2013). Simply fulminating about ancient documents taken out of context is just not adequate for the task. It is interesting how Edward O. Wilson's book *On Human Nature*, for all it will never measure up to the earlier work on human nature by David Hume, does not spark the oxygen-exhausted atmosphere one encounters on reading *The God Delusion* or *The End of Faith*. This is less because Wilson is right and the New Atheists are wrong and more because Wilson is not so much writing against religion, tied to a particular event, but trying to see how religion can be rechanneled in a secular world.

I am not being dismissive. The destruction of the Twin Towers was a truly dreadful act. Thank God, as even a Christian might say, for the moral indignation of the New Atheists. Someone had to respond, and the combined talents of writers like Richard Dawkins and Christopher Hitchens were sorely needed and rose to the challenge. Moreover, as we see shortly, there is much relevant still in the writings of the New Atheists. But let us continue to take the topics in turn.

Which Religion?

An author close to my heart opened his recent book on atheism by saying:

> At the risk of seeming narrow and blinkered – Eurocentric or some such thing – I am going to focus on the atheism debate as it has occurred and continues to occur in the West and those areas of the globe influenced by or settled by the West: Europe, America, other parts of the First World, and places where Western culture predominates. In other words, while recognizing fully and explicitly the debt to Jewish thought, my discussion of atheism is going to be framed within the Christian context. (Ruse 2015, 1)

Who am I to deny the wisdom of such a writer! More seriously, I go on to make the (entirely unoriginal) point that atheism is peculiarly a Western-culture issue. Take Buddhism, for instance. Expanding on what was said in the Prologue, life is ordered hierarchically with layers of beings of different intelligences and sensitivities. Near the bottom, we find petas, wraiths, rather like the Wilis, the jilted maidens one encounters in the second act of *Giselle*. Moving up are animals and then humans. We are not the top, however, for above us are asuras, lesser gods who are not that nice and then devas, greater gods who are a lot nicer. The top gods are the brahmas, and one of them – the Supreme Brahma – works under the mistaken impression that he is the creative force responsible for the world. This he cannot be for, as is well known, there is no such creative force responsible for the world. There is no equivalent to the Abrahamic God, creator and sustainer, who has a special place in his scheme for us humans. In this sense, Buddhism is atheistic, for there is no beginning and no end. Existence just is, in eternity. Yet, as noted in the Prologue, it would surely be deeply misleading to say that the Dalai Lama is an atheist, just as Richard Dawkins and Daniel Dennett are atheists. Spiritually, religiously, they are light-years apart. Edward O. Wilson's attempts to convert Buddhism into a Western religion, notwithstanding, to say simply that Buddhism is atheistic is deeply misleading. When Bertrand Russell spoke of being an atheist, he meant that when he dies, he rots. Game over. That is just not what the Dalai Lama believes.

So we need not hide behind the subject of this Elements series, "monotheism," to focus on the Abrahamic religions. Moreover, it is surely fair for us in the Anglophone world to focus our discussions on Judeo-Christianity. That is the religion – or twin religions – in which we were raised. Given that 9/11 was a function of Muslim beliefs, you might argue – I would argue – that any such discussion today must pay at least some attention to Islam. One can argue that the New Atheists taken as a whole, not to mention Wilson, were not (and could not be expected to be) up to speed on the nature of Islam, as they were presumed to be about Judaism and Christianity. That probably is a fair comment, although it is also fair to note that this is a limitation, not, as Dennett rather implies, a matter of strength. "I am an American writing for Americans, so boo-sucks to the rest of you."

Am I being a little overcautious in offering an argument for not paying equal attention to Buddhism and other religions of the East? Could it be the case that Buddhism is really not a genuine religion, in the sense we are using the word? Fair question. Not everything is a religion. Being a member of the Faculty of Arts and Sciences at Florida State University is not a religious experience, for all that the dean rather fancies himself as God Almighty. However, philosophers have shown in some detail that defining "religion" is a tricky business. You seize on a supposedly central aspect, as that right-angled triangles must have one angle at 90°, and almost at once you run into exceptions. Belief in a God? Leaving the Eastern religions on one side, what about the Unitarians? They certainly get tax relief as religious institutions. What about priests and dogmas? Quakers? Belief in the Trinity? Jehovah's Witnesses and Christadelphians? One God? Mormons? The Bible as the literal word of God? Most Episcopalians? So it goes. Even, especially, ethics. One group is pro-choice and pro-LGBT acceptance. Others are not and would claim that the first group simply has no ethics.

It seems that one must resort to what in the trade is called a cluster or polythetic definition. One names a number of features, none of which is necessary, but a number of which is sufficient. Quakers may not have ministers or dogma, but they are (at least they were when I was a kid) theists accepting Jesus as the son of God. They may not practice holy communion, but that is because they think all of life is sacramental. And while they may not accept Genesis as literal and have little time for substitutionary atonement (Jesus dying on the cross to cancel out the sin of Adam), they accept the Beatitudes literally and have an incarnational theology (Jesus died to set an example of perfect love). Quakerism is a religion in a way that membership in the FSU philosophy department is not. Not much sacramental about our lives. What then of something like Buddhism? Buddhists have priests and set out claims. They have rituals and ways of life. They have a strong moral code, even if, as with Christianity, there are variations. They have an ultimate meaning to life. I see no reason to exclude Buddhists from the family of religions. They seem to have as much right to membership as Unitarians and Quakers. Roman Catholicism is a paradigm example of a religion, scoring positively on just about every criterion, but that does not mean it is a better religion than others, or that others should not enter the fold.

Hatred of Religion

This topic picks up again on the motivation behind New Atheism. 9/11 may have been the spark, but, because it was seen as something evil, the tinder was preprimed by the hatred of religion. If anything, nearly twenty years later the case seems even stronger. The *Boston Globe* uncovered horrendous tales of priestly abuse of the young and vulnerable. The years following have seen a tsunami of similar tales of Catholic priests raping, masturbating, and sodomizing children in country after country, right up the hierarchy to the very top levels. Cardinal Theodore McCarrick, former Archbishop of Washington, has finally been defrocked for what seems to have been an ongoing and blatant practice of abuse of young men, primarily seminarians. Cardinal George Pell, an Australian and until recently the top man in the Vatican for finance, has been found guilty of forcibly demanding oral sex from choir boys found drinking communion wine. There was also a sustained and general pattern of covering up the crimes of priests. Known to be abusers, they were simply moved from one parish to another. That was the stunning revelation of the *Boston Globe* story – how Cardinal Bernard Law was involved in a systematic practice of concealment and deception. One priest alone was able to molest 130 children as he did the circuit of open parishes. Law's punishment? Pope John Paul II appointed him Archpriest of the Basilica di Santa Maria Maggiore in Rome in 2004. He spent his later days fulminating against the requests of the female religious for a more significant role in the Church.

Not that the Catholics are alone. America's largest Protestant denomination is the Southern Baptists. Recently, they too have been rocked by reports of huge numbers of instances of abuse by their clergy. While there is probably no direct cause and effect, it is interesting to note that, like the Catholics, the Southern Baptists are strongly patriarchal. A few years ago, I participated in a debate at one of those megachurches found in the South, this one in Atlanta. I was told proudly that the church has twenty-three pastors. On asking about women, I was told that many women are employed by the church, some even with doctoral qualification. One final question. How many of the pastors are women? The answer? We have not yet felt the call to ordain women. "Let the woman learn in silence with all subjection. But I suffer not a woman to teach, nor to usurp authority over the man, but to be in silence" (1 Timothy 2:11–12). That about says it all.

Except, of course, it doesn't say it all. There is opposition to minorities like gays and lesbians. In this very year (2019), the Methodists decreed that openly homosexual people could not be ministers. St. Paul again. "For this cause God gave them up unto vile affections: for even their women did change the natural use into that which is against nature: And likewise also the men, leaving the natural use of the woman, burned in their lust one toward another; men with men working that which is unseemly, and receiving in themselves that recompence of their error which was meet" (Romans 1:26–27). There is also craven acceptance of the vilest practices of the state, if religion did not start them in the first place. Martin Luther on the subject of Jews comes to mind, and the influence his teaching had right down to the Third Reich, where the churches with few exceptions – the Jehovah's Witnesses was one – went right along with the savage practices of the Nazis and their Führer. Not that others were so very much better. The preaching of prominent Anglicans during the First World War beggars belief. This is a sermon preached in 1915 by Arthur Winnington Ingram, Bishop of London.

> To save the freedom of the world, to save Liberty's own self, to save the honour of women and the innocence of children, everything that is noblest in Europe, everyone that loves freedom and honour, everyone that puts principle above ease, and life itself beyond mere living, are banded in a great crusade – we cannot deny it – to kill Germans: to kill them, not for the sake of killing, but to save the world; to kill the good as well as the bad, to kill the young men as well as the old, to kill those who have shown kindness to our wounded as well as those fiends who crucified the Canadian sergeant, who superintended the Armenian massacres, who sank the *Lusitania*, and who turned the machine-guns on the civilians of Aerschott and Louvain – and to kill them lest the civilisation of the world should itself be killed. (Quoted in Marrin 1974, 175)

So much for the Sermon on the Mount. (See Ruse 2018 for a lot more on this topic.)

I want to make one thing clear. I am not blaming religion for all the ills of the twentieth century. Mao and Stalin did more harm than any predecessor. They were atheists and I do not see their systems as religious. The Nazis are more complex. Religious people supported them and some roots – anti-Semitism for a start – lay in the country's Christian heritage. But, starting with Hitler, Christianity as such was far from a major influence. Turn, however, from defense to offense. Truly, we have had only half the story. Religions, Christianity in particular, have been great forces for moral good. I was raised a Quaker in the years after the Second World War. I have nothing but praise for the loving-kindness of my parents and their coreligionists in the Religious Society of Friends, their strong emphasis on following Jesus' commandments and giving to others, and seeing "that of God in every person." It is not by chance that I have been a lifelong teacher. I also appreciate their equally strong emphasis that everyone must make the major decisions for themselves. There are no easy claims about the nature of existence. It is not by chance that I have been a lifelong philosopher. My Quaker mentors were the descendants of a great tradition of Christian love and service. It was the Quakers, even in the seventeenth century, who first became aware of the evils of slavery. I was raised on stories of the "Quaker saints" like John Woolman, a merchant from Philadelphia, who devoted his life to preaching against the practice of owning and using other human beings. In England, as is well known, Quakers were joined by evangelical members of the established Church of England. Above all, there was William Wilberforce, Member of Parliament and ardent evangelical, driven to his beliefs and actions by his deep Christian faith. The act abolishing slavery throughout the British Empire was passed by Parliament in 1833, three days before his death. Charles Darwin's family, especially on his mother's side, the Wedgwoods – best known of whom is Josiah Wedgwood, founder of the great pottery works – were fanatical antislavery promoters. It is thought that Darwin's older sisters, who raised and nurtured him after the early death of his mother, were ardent evangelicals. The Wedgwoods were Unitarian, another group much involved in the movement.

These were Protestants. What of Catholics? Surely, above all, one thinks of education. The Jesuits are deservedly much celebrated because of their work in secondary and tertiary education. René Descartes, known not only for his invention of analytic geometry but also for his pathbreaking advances in epistemology (theory of knowledge), was famously educated at the Jesuit College at La Flèche in France, where he learned not only mathematics but philosophy also. More recently, in America, the Jesuits have founded an impressive number of colleges and universities – Fordham, Georgetown, Gonzaga, and Marquette, not to mention a handful of Loyolas and others, making a total of twenty-eight. The Society of Jesus is not alone. One thinks, for instance, of the University of Notre Dame in Indiana, founded by the Congregation of the Holy Cross, a French missionary society – for all that the university, especially its football team, is known as the "Irish." Not really so surprising, because the young Catholics in America in the nineteenth century and the early parts of the twentieth were rarely French, and part of the populations of poor immigrants came to the American shores from Ireland and Italy and other countries in Europe. Before they ever got to the upper levels of education, they had been schooled and scolded and shoved by generations of priests and lay brothers and above all nuns and other female religious.

Is religion evil? How long is a piece of string? Some are short, some are long, some are good, some are evil, some are in between. For every naughty vicar, whose habits were revealed in the salacious Sunday newspapers of my childhood – the *News of the World* led the way – there is a Sophie Scholl of the White Rose Group in Munich, who in 1943 went to the guillotine for her open opposition to the Nazi Party. There is much to hate in religion. There is much to love.

Religion a Scientific Question

Here there is general agreement. Science and religion are at war, in competition. Science is going to win, if it has not already done so. Or, in Wilson's somewhat milder version, that which is good in religion is going to be absorbed by science. All of science is in the battle, but Charles Darwin's theory of evolution through natural selection is the key weapon, the atom bomb of the conflict, as one might say. Remember: "the greatest scripture-killer ever penned." And obviously there is much to this. You cannot simultaneously take Genesis literally and *Origin of Species* literally. Either organisms were created miraculously in six days, as Genesis says, or they weren't, as *Origin* says. We should perhaps give people other than Darwin a little more credit. In his *Principles of Geology* (1830–1833), Charles Lyell did sterling service in showing that the earth must be much older than the traditional 6,000 years of the Bible, and he was far from the first. Scottish geologist James Hutton in 1788 said of the world that there was "no vestige of a beginning, no prospect of an end." So much for both Genesis and Revelation.

Few, other than those who have been influenced by the idiosyncratic Protestant religion of 1830s America, are going to be terribly worried by any of this. It was the greatest theologian of the Church, writing around AD 400, who pointed out that, when speaking to the illiterate ancient Jews, God could hardly have used scientific terminology. They were not educated, sophisticated Romans. For instance, Augustine worried that the sun apparently was created on the fourth day (in Genesis 1:16), whereas light had already been around since the first day (in Genesis 1:3). Something has to give, and apparently it is a literal reading of a day as a period of twenty-four hours and of God being limited in such a way – "we should not think either of those days being the ones governed by the sun nor of that working resembling the way that God now works in time" (Augustine 1982). Augustine and subsequent Christian scholars would have stressed that this is not at all to say that the Bible is not true, but that it requires interpretation. A good example of such a way of thinking at work would be proper understanding of the story of Noah's Ark. It is not at all about rain and boat building but about the dangers of simplistic solutions. Everybody is bad so God wipes them all out, except Noah and the other inhabitants of the Ark. And what happens when they get back to dry land? Noah gets stinking drunk and his son laughs at him. Easy answers just don't work. As true a conclusion as any.

For all this, probably some of the reconciliations and reinterpretations are going to be tension-fraught at the very least. Take the already-mentioned doctrine of substitutionary atonement, a key piece of Augustinian theology. Jesus died on the cross to wipe out our sinful nature brought on by the evil act of Adam. But what if, as modern evolutionary biology tells us, there was no unique founding pair, Adam and Eve, that the human species may have gone through bottlenecks but probably there were always 10,000 of us, and that, in any generation, they certainly had parents and grandparents just as good and bad as they were? Sin did not enter the world because of a unique individual sinning for the first time ever (Ruse 2001, 2015). Substitutionary atonement just cannot be right – quite apart from the fact that many of us find it quite morally repellant that God demands an innocent victim to suffer for our sins. If we have done wrong, it is we who should be punished, not Jesus. Think. On the last night in his death cell in Nuremberg, Julius Streicher has a conversion to Christianity and begs forgiveness for his sins. And because Jesus died in agony 2,000 years ago, he is off to heaven. One wonders what he will do when he meets Anne Frank. Oh, sorry! She won't be there because she is a Jew.

In fairness, one should point out that Christians need not resort to ad hoc solutions (Ruse 2019). There is an explanation of the death on the cross that is even more venerable than that of Augustine and that has always been accepted by Eastern churches and many Protestant denominations, like (as already mentioned) the Quakers. Incarnational theory, going back at least to Irenaeus of Lyons, argues that the death is an example of perfect love for us to emulate. Jesus is the supreme example, still with us, encouraging. True, this does not quite have the metaphysical – one might say melodramatic – aspects of atonement theory, but it is an explanation. At which point, I suspect that many atheists would snort with disdain. That is surely the whole point. One is constantly having to water down one's religion in the face of science. One might never show religion impossible, but one makes it so thin as not to be of importance. Why Jesus? Isn't Sophie Scholl at least as good a model of disinterested love and somehow more relevant to our times? His divinity no longer seems so crucial. In a way, Wilson had a point. It is not so much that science disproves religion as that it absorbs the good points and moves on. Disinterested love is important and Darwinian theory tells us why. End of argument.

Religion Not a Scientific Question

Perhaps so, but there is a little more to the story than this. Could it not be that there are some questions that, by their very nature, science cannot explain and that it is open for religion to try its hand? Stephen Jay Gould (1999) spoke of Magisteria, meaning different frameworks by which to view things, frameworks that, rather like Kuhnian paradigms, cannot logically disprove other such frameworks. He argued that science deals with matters of fact and religion deals with matters of morality, and hence the two cannot in principle overlap. No amount of science can get rid of religion. Unfortunately, he rather spoiled his case by adding that religion deals only with morality, which is manifestly false. To say that God exists and that he sent Jesus for our salvation is to make claims about fact, ontological claims. Religion does not want to be purely ethical. Gould's proposal as given just doesn't work.

Can one nevertheless salvage something from the ashes? Start with a point that no one in the debate seems to recognize, namely that scientific theories are anything but pure descriptions of absolutely reality, whatever that is (Ruse 2010). Science is as much interpretation as observation. Science is as dependent on metaphor as is poetry. When I speak of "natural selection," I do not imply a divine selector, rather like an animal breeder. I imply a mechanical process, which I see through the lens of the animal breeder. And this leads me on heuristically. Breeders go for certain valuable features, like wool and meaty haunches. Does nature also go for certain valuable features, like ferocity and toughness? More broadly, bringing together particular metaphors – force, pressure, attraction, natural selection, selfish gene – science is governed by what linguists call "root" metaphors, overarching perspectives on reality (Lakoff and Johnson 1980). Until the Scientific Revolution, one saw the world as an organism (Ruse 2013). Even (especially) something like the earth was seen in organic terms, with growth (spring), flourishing (summer), decay (fall), and death (winter). Kepler of all people tells us that:

> As the body displays tears, mucus, and earwax, and also in places lymph from pustules on the face, so the Earth displays amber and bitumen; as the bladder pours out urine, so the mountains pour out rivers; as the body produces excrement of sulphurous odor and farts which can even be set on fire, so the Earth produces sulphur, subterranean fires, thunder, and lightning; and as blood is generated in the veins of an animate being, and with it sweat, which is thrust outside the body, so in the veins of the Earth are generated metals and fossils, and rainy vapor. (1977, 363–364)

Then came the change from organism to machine, the root metaphor of modern science. We see the world in a mechanical fashion. Robert Boyle, the seventeenth-century philosopher-chemist, argued that the world is "like a rare clock, such as may be that at Strasbourg, where all things are so skillfully contrived that the engine being once set a-moving, all things proceed according to the artificer's first design, and the motions of the little statues that at such hours perform these or those motions do not require (like those of puppets) the peculiar interposing of the artificer or any intelligent agent employed by him, but perform their functions on particular occasions by virtue of the general and primitive contrivance of the whole engine" ([1688]1966, 12–13).

Now consider what this means. As Thomas Kuhn (1993) saw, and emphasized in his later writings, metaphors are paradigms or at least function very much like paradigms. They give you a conceptual scheme and point to new directions of research, but they do all of this by restricting inquiry. To use another metaphor, they do this by putting blinders around scientists' eyes. Consider "my love is like a red, red rose" and make a metaphor of it. It means that we see the love as beautiful, fresh, desirable. If we are joking, it means that perhaps she is a little bit prickly. What we say nothing about is whether she is Protestant or Catholic, good at mathematics or just plain dumb. These are genuine questions, but not within the domain of this metaphor, which is a good thing. Likewise, if you are considering, let us say, a problem in island geography, it matters where on the globe one finds the islands – close to the Pacific or close to the Atlantic. As a scientist, you are not going to waste time worrying about whether you can see more eclipses from the Galapagos than from the Azores. Of course, you might say the relative number of visible eclipses was a function of the geography, but the eclipses are surely not a factor in there being giant tortoises on the Galapagos and not the Azores. With possible qualifications, like long-distance bird routes, you are not going to spend your time on astronomy. You are going to spend your time working out the mechanics of crossing the sea and that sort of thing.

What's this adding up to? Simply, that the machine metaphor of modern science – mechanism – excludes certain questions from consideration. Here are four. Why is there something rather than nothing? What is the justification of morality? What is mind? What does it all mean? There may be others, but these will do for a start. Remember, I am not arguing that there are no answers to these questions or that the questions are not genuine, just that the machine metaphor doesn't even attempt to answer them. Take them in turn. First, of course you can ask where something came from. The ancestral tortoises came from South America. But going back, in the end, you just take existence as a given. It is like the cookbook says. First, take your hare. Second, morality. We have more to say about this shortly, including the claim that morality has no justification. But if you demand justification, you are not going to find it in science. David Hume ([1739–1740]1978) made that clear. There is a logical distinction between claims of fact – "is" statements – and claims of morality – "ought" statements. Is the guillotine a good thing? I would say no. I suspect most Floridians would say yes, enthusiastically. Third, the body-mind problem. I am right with Leibniz on this. Machines don't think.

One is obliged to admit that *perception* and what depends upon it is *inexplicable on mechanical principles*, that is, by figures and motions. In imagining that there is a machine whose construction would enable it to think, to sense, and to have perception, one could conceive it enlarged while retaining the same proportions, so that one could enter into it, just like into a windmill. Supposing this, one should, when visiting within it, find only parts pushing one another, and never anything by which to explain a perception. Thus it is in the simple substance, and not in the composite or in the machine, that one must look for perception. (Leibniz 1714, 215)

Fourth, ultimate meaning. Nobel Laureate Steven Weinberg wrote: "The more the universe seems comprehensible, the more it also seems pointless" (1977, 154). Why am I not surprised? Simply because the machine metaphor does not ask questions of meaning. It just deals with systems in motion (or at rest) governed by unchanging, unbreakable laws. You might complain that machines do have meaning. Guillotines are for chopping off heads and a very good thing too. However, in the machine metaphor of science, those questions have been dropped. Go back to my love and her rose-like nature. My roses thrive on Day-Glo. I am not suggesting that my love would be improved by a little bit of ground-up cow manure. The metaphor is restricted. As historians have noted, the meaning question was found unhelpful and dropped.

> No Christian could ultimately escape the implications of the fact that Aristotle's cosmos knew no Jehovah. Christianity taught him to see it as a divine artifact, rather than as a self-contained organism. The universe was subject to God's laws; its regularities and harmonies were divinely planned; its uniformity was a result of providential design. The ultimate mystery resided in God rather than in Nature, which could thus, by successive steps, be seen not as a self-sufficient Whole but as a divinely organized machine in which was transacted the unique drama of the Fall and Redemption. If an omnipresent God was all spirit, it was all the more easy to think of the physical universe as all matter; the intelligences, spirits, and Forms of Aristotle were first debased and then abandoned as unnecessary in a universe that contained nothing but God, human souls, and matter. (Hall 1954, xvi–xvii)

Ultimate meaning was no longer part of science.

I argue that at least these four questions are unanswered by science because they are unasked by science. As an obvious corollary, I argue that it is proper for religion to try to answer them, as it does. Why is there something rather than nothing? Because a good God made it all. What is the foundation of morality? God's will. What is mind? That which makes us in the image of God, able to think and respond morally. What is the meaning of it all? Eternal bliss with our Creator. Note that I am not saying that religion can answer them successfully, and obviously there are going to be scientific-type questions that religion will not answer, about the mind-body relationship, for instance. Perhaps a different science root metaphor will be more successful, or perhaps – as many have argued – we need to go back to the organic metaphor. These are different questions, some of which are answered shortly. The point here is simply that science does not necessarily answer all questions and there are some that it is still legitimate for religion to tackle.

4 Critique Continued

God's Existence

The first thing demanded of someone like me, a professional philosopher, is to take a deep breath and vow not to get too irritated by the contempt shown toward philosophy, especially when it gets involved in arguments for and against God's existence. Another of the New Atheist sidekicks, Arizona State University physics professor Laurence Krauss, excels at this. "Philosophy is a field that, unfortunately, reminds me of that old Woody Allen joke, 'those that can't do, teach, and those that can't teach, teach gym.'" One should add, in amelioration, that he had just been roughed up rather badly in the *New York Times* book review section by a professor of philosophy at Columbia University. That chap, apparently, was so stupid as to be considered "moronic" (LeDrew 2016, 83). Richard Dawkins, as we have seen, is pretty good at this kind of game, and even Daniel Dennett does not seem overly enamored with his fellow philosophers – although, with perhaps more justification than he intended, one might argue that, in *Breaking the Spell*, he is not really writing as a professional philosopher.

Let me, as a philosopher, say this about the arguments for the existence of God. With exceptions, many Thomist philosophers, for instance, most (not all) philosophers today doubt that the arguments are fully valid. Accept the premises and you must accept the God of the Abrahamic tradition. As Kant made clear – Gaunilo long before him (who, when Anselm wrote criticizing the fool who hath said there is no God, at once wrote on behalf of the fool!), there are lots of problems with considering existence as a predicate – a property like green or solid or beautiful – which is a crucial presupposition of the ontological argument. The causal or cosmological argument does have all sorts of problems, starting with the worry that in this age of quantum mechanics, causation seems nothing like what was once assumed – is every quantum effect caused in the same way as a hammer on wood causes a banging sound? And this is before we get into traditional issues about the causation of God Himself. I should say, though, that I doubt most philosophers would be much impressed by Dawkins's arguments about complexity, that a simple God could not produce the intricate universe. We get complexity out of simplicity all the time. Think Euclidean geometry, with the simple premises and the complex theorems.

The teleological argument does seem a bit hollow after Darwin (Ruse 2017). What need have we of God when we have natural selection? Moreover, when we turn to other arguments, they seem no better. The argument from miracles was roughed up by David Hume. It is always more reasonable to believe that something has been missaid or lied about than a violation of the laws of nature. Do you really think that Jesus turned water into wine, or that the host shamed by

Jesus' rebuke went down to his cellar and got out the good stuff? Honestly, do you truly believe in the miracles rustled up for the sainthoods of John Paul II and Mother Teresa and others?

What about going the other way? What about the problem of evil, supposedly showing that the God of the Bible cannot possibly exist? An all-loving, all-powerful God could not possibly have created such a world as ours with so much pain and suffering. Interestingly, the New Atheists seem relatively indifferent to this. Dawkins (2006) goes so far as to say that the judgment that the existence of such calamities as earthquakes "counts strongly against the likelihood that God exists" is a "judgement opposite to mine" (108). Dawkins simply supposes an evil God, which one assumes does do the trick but which seems not much to the point. The point is whether evil destroys the possibility of a good God. As it happens, although they do not share the complacency of Dawkins, and certainly want the argument cast in terms of the biblical God, many philosophers today are inclined to think with him that the argument from evil is no big problem. It is argued that there are two kinds of evil, moral evil – Heinrich Himmler – and natural evil – the Lisbon earthquake. To speak to the first, we have the claim that moral evil demands free will and this is an ultimate and justifying good, and to speak to the second, we have the Leibnizian argument that God cannot do the impossible and natural evil is a consequence of a world like ours. God made the best of all possible worlds, for all that Voltaire parodied the idea in *Candide*.

At this level, I am inclined to agree with these philosophers (Ruse 2001). Interestingly, and perhaps paradoxically, Darwinian evolutionary theory offers support. If you accept a compatibilist view of free will, namely that it can (and must) occur within a deterministic system, then note that it is a crucial part of the Darwinian view of humankind that we have so advanced that we have a degree of autonomy not possessed by most other organisms, if any at all. Most organisms, if faced with a problem, let us say a tornado, are helpless in its path. Humans are like the Mars Rover (an analogy of Dennett's). Faced with a threat, we can respond and try to solve the problem, by dashing into a cave, for instance. We are free in a way that most organisms are not. With respect to natural evil, Richard Dawkins (1983) of all people has backed the Leibnizian argument, saying that if we are to have complex functioning organisms, then only natural selection can do the job, and this means pain and suffering. Obviously, natural selection is not the only cause of pain and suffering, but it is a good start.

Does this mean that natural theology is all a bit of a draw? It doesn't really prove anything absolute one way or the other, but it does draw attention to some interesting and important questions. The ontological argument may not be valid, but it does set you to thinking about the nature of existence. Is all existence contingent – Julius Caesar existed but he might not have – or can it in some sense be necessary, like mathematics or the laws of logic? What is the nature of cause? Are all causes the same? Does it make sense to speak of something being the cause of itself, and would its necessity be the same as that of logic? The hand and the eye really do seem to be as if designed. If they were not, then what natural processes might there be? How can we counter the Second Law of Thermodynamics, that things are always running down? What is the nature of free will? Does Darwinism throw any light on it? Is Darwinian mechanism the only way to get design effects?

In respects, I think this two-way conclusion – natural theology may not work as it should but it is revealingly important – is true. But one more point must be made. Certainly, within the Christian tradition, natural theology has never been primary. Revealed theology has always been the starting point (Ruse 2019). John Henry Newman said it all. "I believe in design because I believe in God; not in a God because I see design" (1973, 97). He continues: "Design teaches me power, skill and goodness – not sanctity, not mercy, not a future judgment, which three are of the essence of religion." Let us see where this insight leads us.

Faith

"Now faith is the substance of things hoped for, the evidence of things not seen" (Hebrews 11:1). Many modern theologians, for instance the hugely influential Karl Barth, much in the tradition of Søren Kierkegaard, stress that religious belief comes down to a matter of faith. Hardly a new thought. We have seen already how Jesus roughed up Thomas when he asked for proof that Jesus arisen was really Jesus – "blessed are they that have not seen, and yet have believed" (John 20:29). What of Aquinas, man of the five proofs? He did think that reason could be effective. "For certain things that are true about God wholly surpass the capability of human reason, for instance that God is three and one: while there are certain things to which even natural reason can attain, for instance that God is, that God is one, and others like these" (Aquinas 1952, 5). At the same time, note, as was said earlier, he is giving the ultimate role to faith. Without faith, your understanding is limited. Aquinas pointed out that, without faith being all powerful, there would be no knowledge of God for the ignorant and stupid and lazy. We saw that the very conservative John Paul II, in his encyclical *Fides et Ratio*, endorsed this thinking entirely.

Now, what about the critique of the New Atheists? Faith is without foundation, it is a sign of weakness or stupidity or cowardice. "Faith is an evil precisely because it requires no justification and brooks no argument." In the same vein:

"Faith is what credulity becomes when it finally achieves escape velocity from the constraints of terrestrial discourse – constraints like reasonableness, internal coherence, civility, and candor" (Harris 2004, 65). "'Knowledge' acquired by religion is at odds not only with scientific knowledge, but also with knowledge professed by other religions. In the end, religion's methods, unlike those of science, are useless for understanding reality" (64). And so on, at great length. Let us, however, take pause, because people of faith are not all moronic, to use Lawrence Krauss's favorite word. People of faith are not alcoholics seeing pink rats run up the wall. They tell us that they have had overwhelming experiences, convincing them of the truths of religion. Thus, John Hick, noted philosopher of religion and prime mover in interfaith discussions in the British Midlands city of Birmingham. "An experience of this kind which I cannot forget, even though it happened forty-two years ago [1942], occurred – of all places – on the top deck of a bus in the middle of the city of Hull . . . As everyone will be very conscious who can themselves remember such a moment, all descriptions are inadequate. But it was as though the skies opened up and light poured down and filled me with a sense of overflowing joy, in response to an immense transcendent good-ness and love" (2005).

All of us have had similar experiences. This is David Copperfield, in Charles Dickens's novel of that name.

> We turned into a room near at hand ... and I heard a voice say, "Mr. Copperfield, my daughter Dora, and my daughter Dora's confidential friend!" It was, no doubt, Mr. Spenlow's voice, but I didn't know it, and I didn't care whose it was. All was over in a moment. I had fulfilled my destiny. I was a captive and a slave. I loved Dora Spenlow to distraction!
>
> She was more than human to me. She was a Fairy, a Sylph, I don't know what she was – anything that no one ever saw, and everything that every-body ever wanted. I was swallowed up in an abyss of love in an instant. There was no pausing on the brink; no looking down, or looking back; I was gone, headlong, before I had sense to say a word to her. (Dickens [1850] 1948, 390)

You might say that there is a big difference between falling in love and religious faith. In the former case, you know that it is a subjective feeling, peculiar to you. Others may not feel the same way. You probably hope that they don't. But religious faith claims to be true, to be knowledge, and is something about which nonbelievers are wrong. Well, yes, but note that religious faith is not like believing in pink rats running up the wall. That is a scientific claim and is wrong. Faith is about things beyond science, like an ultimate Creator and the Trinity and life after death. It doesn't mean it cannot be challenged, but it cannot be challenged simply because it is not science. And the fact is we do have powerful emotions, that we think good, that take us beyond the evidence, as in David's conviction that Dora was the most wonderful human being in the world. But can faith and its conclusions be challenged? Yes, I think they can be, but this must be on their own terms, or rather, since people who don't have faith cannot use faith to challenge faith, on terms using reason and evidence that try to attack the claims. These are the only terms available to them and unless you say that faith cannot be challenged because it is self-validating – an unattractive option to those who do not have faith and who are probably inclined to think some element of self-delusion is at work – it is legitimate to move forward.

For myself, three factors make me very uncomfortable to accept faith, especially in any Christian context. First, to go back to the problem of evil, even if we grant free will is important, I simply want no part of a God who prized the free will of Heinrich Himmler over the life and happiness of Anne Frank. I am with Dostoevsky on this one. In the *Brothers Karamazov*, Ivan asks Alyosha a question:

> "Tell me yourself, I challenge your answer. Imagine that you are creating a fabric of human destiny with the object of making men happy in the end, giving them peace and rest at last, but that it was essential and inevitable to torture to death only one tiny creature – that baby beating its breast with its fist, for instance – and to found that edifice on its unavenged tears, would you consent to be the architect on those conditions? Tell me, and tell the truth."
>
> "No, I wouldn't consent," said Alyosha softly. (Dostoevsky [1879–1880] 2003)

Second, there is the problem of different faiths. I grew up a Quaker so I believed in one kind of God. Had I grown up a Jew in the Pale of Settlement in the nineteenth century, I would have perhaps believed in the same God, but honestly a very different kind of God – not a Trinity, for a start. Had I grown up a Mormon, different again. And so it goes. Why my God, who is different from His creation, rather than the Gaia-like force of the pagans who is pantheistic? Or why a Creator God at all, if I were a Buddhist? John Hick opts for some kind of religious pluralism:

> Let us begin with the recognition, which is made in all the main religious traditions, that the ultimate divine reality is infinite and as such transcends the grasp of the human mind. God, to use our Christian term, is infinite. He is not a thing, a part of the universe, existing alongside other things; nor is he a being falling under a certain kind. And therefore, he cannot be defined or encompassed by human thought. We cannot draw boundaries around his nature and say he is this and no more. If we could fully define God, describing his inner being and his outer limits, this would not be God. The God whom

our minds can penetrate and whom our thoughts can circumnavigate is merely a finite and partial image of God. (1973, 139)

To use the familiar metaphor of the blind men and the elephant, we give different accounts of the elephant as we see or encounter it, but in the end it is the same elephant. It is just that our knowledge is limited.

Perhaps, but I am really not sure that most Christians are going to give up the Trinity that easily. Which brings me to the third problem I have with Christianity. It is an uneasy amalgam of Greek thought – particularly thanks to Augustine of Platonic thought, with God identified with the Form of the Good, outside time and space – and Jewish thought, with God as a person – the God who walks in the cool of the evening and who cherishes the newly returned son while comforting the sensible son. You can paper over it, but the cracks are still there (Ruse 2015). Greek: "Thy years are but a day, and thy day is not recurrent, but always today." Jewish: "Theism postulates God as a person with intentions, beliefs, and basic powers." All of this leads to some horrible consequences. Aquinas of all people states that: "To sorrow, therefore, over the misery of others does not belong to God" (1952, I, 21, 3).

I am not sure that having faith is as crazy as the New Atheists make it out to be, but I don't have faith and I am not striving to have it.

Why Religion?

If you are a believer, then presumably your religion is true and your Maker has set things up so that you can find it, understand it, and believe it. If you are not a believer, then clearly you must think it some kind of illusion or even delusion. Hume is the starting point here. "We find human faces in the moon, armies in the clouds; and by a natural propensity, if not corrected by experience and reflection, ascribe malice or good-will to everything, that hurts or pleases us" (Hume [1757]1963, 78). It is easy to move on to an evolutionary scenario. As Dawkins said, it is all a by-product. Thus Darwin, who argued that the "tendency in savages to imagine that natural objects and agencies are animated by spiritual or living essences" was illustrated by the mistaken actions of his dog. Sleeping on the lawn, the dog was upset by a parasol moving in the wind. Going on the attack "every time that the parasol slightly moved, the dog growled fiercely and barked. He must, I think, have reasoned to himself in a rapid and unconscious manner, that movement without any apparent cause indicated the presence of some strange living agent, and that no stranger had a right to be on his territory" (Darwin 1871, 1, 67).

Of course, there is no reason why something that first appears by chance or as a by-product should not then be picked up for adaptive reasons – or what appears for one adaptive reason taken over for another. Did women's breasts first appear to feed infants or to attract males? So, subject to empirical confirmation, I see no reason why religions should not have the kinds of evolutionary virtues that Edward O. Wilson associates with them. (Note that I say "evolutionary virtues," not that they are necessarily good things in themselves. I can think of many cases where they are not.) Of course, the evolutionist as an explainer does not really care what form the religion takes. From a biological viewpoint, Islam is probably as good as Christianity. By any reasonable standard, Mormonism is a bit odd – but it obviously works. Is the Christian or other believer therefore committed to some kind of theistic evolution, where God guarantees that we arrive at the right place? Different Gods for different faiths! You might try the gambit of appealing to multiverses. Given infinite time and space, something apparently possessed by God, sometime, somewhere some group of human-like beings is bound to hit on the truth. The fact that we happen to have won the jackpot is just a fact, as someone must win any jackpot. Of course, this does rather mean that the multiverses are littered with folk who did not buy a winning ticket. They believe in false gods. Since those down on Planet Earth already believe that of those here who have other beliefs, I suppose that the extraterrestrial losers are only to be expected – pitied perhaps, damned certainly.

Ethics

Morality has been an obsession of nonbelievers right from the start. The age of Darwin just added fuel to the flames. After nonbelieving novelist George Eliot's death, an acquaintance said this of her.

> I remember how, at Cambridge, I walked with her once in the Fellows' Garden of Trinity, on an evening of rainy May; and she, stirred somewhat beyond her wont, and taking as her text the three words which have been used so often as the inspiring trumpet-calls of men – the words God, Immortality, Duty – pronounced, with terrible earnestness, how inconceivable was the first, how unbelievable the second, and yet how peremptory and absolute the third. Never perhaps have sterner accents affirmed the sovereignty of impersonal and unrecompensing Law. I listened, and night fell; her grave, majestic countenance turned toward me like a sibyl's in the gloom; it was as though she withdrew from my grasp, one by one, the two scrolls of promise, and left me the third scroll only, awful with inevitable fates. And when we stood at length and parted amid that columnar circuit of the forest trees, beneath the last twilight of starless skies, I seemed to be gazing, like Titus at Jerusalem, on vacant seats and empty halls – on a sanctuary with no Presence to hallow it, and heaven left lonely of a God. (Myers 1881, 47)

None of the evolutionists had any doubt that morality emerged naturally from the evolutionary process. Darwin, expectedly, put it all down to natural selection. "There can be no doubt that a tribe including many members who, from possessing in a high degree the spirit of patriotism, fidelity, obedience, courage, and sympathy, were always ready to give aid to each other and to sacrifice themselves for the common good, would be victorious over most other tribes; and this would be natural selection." Hence: "At all times throughout the world tribes have supplanted other tribes; and as morality is one element in their success, the standard of morality and the number of well-endowed men will thus everywhere tend to rise and increase" (Darwin 1871, 1, 166). Basically, with some variations, this is where we stand today.

Parenthetically, the variations usually devolve on the so-called units of selection controversy (Richards and Ruse 2016). Is selection always for the individual – "selfish genes" – or can it be for the group? Alfred Russel Wallace believed in group selection, but Darwin was ever strong for individual selection. Given the talk just presented about "tribes," it seems that he was at times a group selectionist, but he made clear that he regarded tribes as groups of related individuals, or who think they are related. Hence, he accepted a proto-form of what is now known as "kin selection." Today, most evolutionists are individual selectionists through and through. They are not hard-line libertarians. They just don't think group selection works. Controversially, Edward O. Wilson in recent years has swung strongly to a group-selection perspective. Not Dawkins!

What about the justification of morality, what we philosophers call metaethics? A lot of evolutionists – in the past, Herbert Spencer (1857) most notably and today, Edward O. Wilson (1975) equally notably – think that evolution is progressive, from the blob to the primate, from the monad to the man (Ruse 1996). Dawkins is likewise an enthusiast. Hence, since progress is good, what has evolved at the top – humankind – is the supreme good. Morally, therefore, we are justified in cherishing humans and seeing that they do not regress. Canadian sociologist Stephen LeDrew (2016) makes much of this progressionism and argues that it is the backbone of the ideological nature of New Atheism. Writing of this movement, he claims: "The key idea within this ideology is the evolution of society from the premodern phase of religious superstition to the modern phase characterized by scientism and its application to social and political questions and problems. This involves a teleological vision of human progress, with 'premodern' giving way to 'modern' ways of thinking and living" (59). He ties this in with the claim that the New Atheist movement is essentially a right-wing movement, with much in common with right-wing evangelicals, in privileging the European way of life.

I agree in major respects with this characterization. Right at the beginning of this Element, I spoke of the ethical factors underlying debates and claims. Also, as you have just seen, I accept the significance of ideas of progress in all of this. Even the claim about Eurocentrism has merit. Listen to Charles Darwin. "The more civilised so-called Caucasian races have beaten the Turkish hollow in the struggle for existence. Looking to the world at no very distant date, what an endless number of the lower races will have been eliminated by the higher civilised races throughout the world" (Letter 13230, Darwin Correspondence Project, to William Graham, July 3, 1881). Adding a little nuance, right-wing Christians also criticize our culture, arguing, for instance, that it is too tolerant of women's rights – they allow no female preachers – and, as we have seen, Intelligent Design Theory (Creationism-lite) founder Phillip Johnson is obsessed about cross-dressing as a metaphor for feminism. Richard Dawkins is little better. This is from a letter to an imaginary Muslim woman.

> Stop whining, will you. Yes, yes, I know you had your genitals mutilated with a razor blade, and … yawn … don't tell me yet again, I know you aren't allowed to drive a car, and you can't leave the house without a male relative, and your husband is allowed to beat you, and you'll be stoned to death if you commit adultery. But stop whining, will you. Think of the suffering your poor American sisters have to put up with. (LeDrew 2016, 199, quoting from a blog entry of 2011)

This said, without at all condoning Johnson or Dawkins – or Darwin, for that matter – being Eurocentric in many respects is hardly offensively ideological. I cherish science and Europe (and America) are the places for science. I would far rather live in a country that celebrates the Salk polio vaccine than a place like Pakistan where health workers can be killed for trying to force such Western products on the children of the country. Paradoxically, I would say it is precisely the science of the West that shows us that women are not inferior or that (to take another example) gays are perverts (Ruse 2012). Dawkins betrays his own ideology.

What of progress, focusing now on the New Atheists' need of progress, rather than the claim (accepted) that progress is central to their position? Is evolution – Darwinian evolution – so very progressive? From the perspective of natural selection, brains are high-maintenance objects, needing lots of high-quality fuel, meaning the bodies of other animals. At times, however, being a vegan might be a better reproductive strategy. It all depends on what is available and, from this, different adaptations evolve. Paleontologist John ("Jack") Sepkoski put the point graphically and humorously. "I see intelligence as just one of a variety of adaptations among tetrapods for survival. Running fast in a herd

while being as dumb as shit, I think, is a very good adaptation for survival"
(Ruse 1996, 486).

What other options might one take? As a committed Darwinian, I am
inclined to a form of moral nonrealism (Ruse and Richards 2017). In what
is known today as the "debunking argument," I suggest that evolution is
what works and there is no ultimate justification for morality. We could
have evolved in a different way with a quite different moral code. Darwin
(1871) saw this.

> If, for instance, to take an extreme case, men were reared under precisely the
> same conditions as hive-bees, there can hardly be a doubt that our unmarried
> females would, like the worker-bees, think it a sacred duty to kill their
> brothers, and mothers would strive to kill their fertile daughters; and no one
> would think of interfering. Nevertheless the bee, or any other social animal,
> would in our supposed case gain, as it appears to me, some feeling of right and
> wrong, or a conscience. (1, 73)

As with most of my forays into regular philosophical thinking, people don't find
terribly convincing the kinds of conclusions I endorse. I will just leave things by
saying I see no reason for religious underpinning to morality. Perhaps God does
stand behind morality. We would still be moral even if He decided to spend the
rest of eternity drinking coffee in Starbucks.

Children

There is still the question of whether religion itself is immoral. Things can be
said on both sides. Religion has led to some very bad things. It has led to some
very good things. I am not at all convinced that Hitler's childhood Catholicism
led to his vile social beliefs. He certainly believed in a supernatural force –
destiny or some such thing – but generally he was pretty contemptuous of
Christian religion, about on a par with his attitude to evolution that insists we
Arians are cousins of the Jews. I find these sorts of general discussions – religion
good? religion bad? – long and tedious and usually not fruitful. Let us get more
specific, wrapping up the discussion with looking at the controversial topic of
children. To his credit, it is Jerry Coyne who fulminates most about the evils of
religion's role in the physical mistreatment of children – denying them proper
medical care and so forth. Often, to be honest, it is difficult to distinguish
philosophy from religion at these times, but the ill effects are the same. As
one who grew up when swimming pools were often closed in the summer and
when classmates (not to mention presidents) lived in wheelchairs, once again,
I can only thank God for the polio vaccine – or Dr. Salk, which in my book is
much the same.

I have a stake in all of this. I was born in 1940 and got most of the childhood illnesses like measles and chickenpox and mumps. Vaccinations were only coming to their full power in my early days. My wife (twenty years younger than I) and all my children have been fully vaccinated and had none of these ailments. When I was an early teenager, my young mother died suddenly and on the rebound my father married a German woman whose family were much into so-called anthroposophy, a variant of theosophy, started by Austrian guru Rudolf Steiner. Best known from the movement are Waldorf schools, the first of which Steiner designed for a rich cigarette manufacturer, and for more than thirty years my father worked at such a school in the south of England. Amongst other things, the Steiner movement – which has a religious offshoot called the "Christian Community" – is strongly against vaccination, because Dr. Steiner (his doctorate was a PhD) believed that childhood illnesses are a natural part of development. Today, Waldorf schools are much in the news because so few of the children are vaccinated and inevitably welcoming homes of illnesses like measles, which, unstopped, spread like wildfire. My father had 25 percent strength in one eye and 50 percent in the other eye. For thirty years, he sworn blind – an appropriate metaphor – that childhood illnesses are an important part of growth. I don't think I am being particularly Oedipal in saying that I hate the anti-vax movement.

What about the kind of evil on which Richard Dawkins focuses – bringing children up with religious faith? Here surely the answer must be more nuanced. Anyone who brings up children as extreme anti-Semites is doing a terrible thing, irrespective of whether it is done in the name of religion. And if this systematically leads to violence, then strong measures should be taken to counter it and such like indoctrinations. I am not sure, though, that I would follow Harris in bumping off the worst offenders before they become too active. But what about religions like the Catholics and Baptists that have at their hearts – denials notwithstanding – the belief that women are in some sense inferior, not as good as men? I don't like them, any more than I like the Tea Party. I can write against them, as I am doing now. I am not sure that, in a free society, there is more I can or should do. Freedom only really has bite when you let people do things of which you disapprove. What about any kind of religion? I feel much the same kind of way that I feel about politics. I am not a conservative. I find it hard to say that John McCain was a bad man for being a conservative or for bringing up his children to think as he did politically. What about people more liberal, like myself? People who think that not to have some form of national health service is stupid and immoral? Should people all be raised to be blank slates on these sorts of issues, making decisions only after they have taken a couple of classes of philosophy? Surely not. I feel the same about religion. I am extremely grateful for my Quaker upbringing. I feel I have lived a better and more fulfilling life because of it. It is not by chance that I am now in my fifty-fourth year of being a teacher. I think the same can be said of many of my contemporaries – my friends and my wife's friends. Some of our deepest friendships started because of children of the same age in the same classes or using the same park playground. My wife's closest friend is the director of Christian education at the major Presbyterian church here in town. I think she is a good woman and I think it was a good thing that she raised her children in her faith. So, in the end, I guess, although a nonbeliever I am more with Wilson than with Dawkins. I can live with that.

Conclusion

Are the New Atheists a good thing or a bad thing, are they right or are they wrong? There is a famous (1895) cartoon from the English humorous magazine *Punch*, showing a curate at breakfast with his bishop. The bishop turns to the younger man, concerned, and comments: "I'm afraid you've got a bad Egg, Mr. Jones!" To which the curate replies: "Oh no, my Lord, I assure you! Parts of it are excellent!" That is how I feel about the New Atheists. They make some excellent points, and they write with great power and conviction. However, many of their arguments are simply not well taken. Through ignorance, carelessness, inability I leave others to assess. Overall? Curate's egg!

Epilogue: Darwinian Existentialism

Existence Precedes Essence

In this Epilogue, I offer some thoughts of my own on the topic of this Element. Since this is really an Element on atheism and not on Michael Ruse, I will try to be atypically short. Apart from anything else, I am not really an atheist. At least, I am about most religions – resurrection from the dead and that sort of thing – but I am more agnostic or skeptic. In Stephen LeDrew's terminology, I am a "humanist" rather than an "atheist." Although humanists are in the no God business, their central concern is with social issues, as against atheists for whom the denial of God is all important. In Victorian times, secularist George Jacob Holyoake, who was a founder of the Co-op movement, opposed militant atheist Charles Bradlaugh, noted already as the first overt atheist to sit in the British Parliament. Today, philosopher Philip Kitcher (2014) stands against biologist Richard Dawkins (2006). Humanists can form bonds with some religious people; atheists cannot. So I do have justification over self-promotion for presenting my position as a contrast to the New Atheist. How does a humanist see things? As a footnote, I should explain that I don't much care for being called a "humanist," for that – like the Unitarians – rather implies that I am making a religion from my position. Having given up one religion, I am not about to take up another. Mine is more a metaphysical world picture. I don't tie pink ribbons on oak trees to protest the rape of the environment.

I just don't know if there is any ultimate meaning – or Meaning, as one might say. More importantly, I make a virtue out of what Hardy found as terrifyingly upsetting. I don't care whether there is a God and whether He/She/ It gives a damn about us. We are on our own, and we must make m/Meaning for ourselves (Ruse 2019). In the spirit of Jean-Paul Sartre, I call myself an "existentialist."

> Existentialism is not so much an atheism in the sense that it would exhaust itself attempting to demonstrate the nonexistence of God; rather, it affirms that even if God were to exist, it would make no difference – that is our point of view. It is not that we believe that God exists, but we think that the real problem is not one of his existence; what man needs is to rediscover himself and to comprehend that nothing can save him from himself, not even valid proof of the existence of God. (Sartre 1948, 56, based on a lecture given in 1945)

Unpacking:

> My atheist existentialism … declares that God does not exist, yet there is still a being in whom existence precedes essence, a being which exists before being defined by any concept, and this being is man or, as Heidegger puts it, human reality. That means that man first exists, encounters himself and emerges in the world, to be defined afterwards. Thus, there is no human nature, since there is no God to conceive it. It is man who conceives himself, who propels himself towards existence. Man becomes nothing other than what is actually done, not what he will want to be. (27–28)

We are here and we are on our own. Life is what we make of it. There is no divine admissions officer looking over our life's transcripts to see if we qualify for an Ivy League of heavenly eternity. You may think I am being a little two-faced here, because I have admitted that there are ultimate questions that are unanswered by science – why is there something rather than nothing, what is the foundation of morality, what is mind and its relation to body, and what does it all mean and lead to? As you now know, I think religion has the right to try to answer, and as you also know, I am not that taken with religion's answers. I am prepared to say that perhaps there is no reason for existence, it just is; perhaps there is no ultimate justification for morality, it is an illusion put in place by our genes to make us cooperators (Ruse and Wilson 1986) – the only gem that Michael Ruse will ever get into the *Oxford Book of Quotations*; perhaps like quantum mechanics – wave or particle? – the nature of mind will forever be beyond our grasp; and there simply is no reason for it all. Again, it just is and, when for us it is over, it is over. We are here and we are on our own.

Human Nature

At the risk of losing my place in the hall of great modern thinkers, I do disagree with Sartre about there being no human nature. I don't think you need God to get it. Darwinian evolutionary theory does a pretty good job. Evolution divides organisms up into species – Darwin's division of labor – and these groups or species are morphologically and behaviorally and genetically different from other groups. They have their own adaptive virtues and limits. In the case of humans, obviously, being bipedal and rational is a good start. One expects and finds that there will be exceptions and borderline cases in nigh every group. Humans are no different. Humans are male or female to such an extent that one can say that this is one of the distinguishing factors about humans. There are intersexes, but the numbers are so few as to make little difference to the overall judgment. There is such variation in skin color that no one would say a distinguishing characteristic is that we are white or black – although generally we are not blue or green. Whatever the color, we have skin and are relatively hairless. I realize that the notion of human nature is (as one might say) much contested, usually for moral reasons, rather than scientific. Many gays and lesbians are not that keen on the notion, for it seems to exclude them. It's an understandable worry, but it is not a fatal objection. A gay man or a lesbian woman is just as much a human as a person with blue eyes – they are all around or below the 10 percent mark. And for what it is worth, there are all sorts of good biological reasons why homosexual orientation might be adaptive, directly or indirectly through kin (Ruse 1988b, 2012).

Now, if we do have a human nature, where is the existential part of all of this? I want to say that we start with our human nature – our existence – and then we go on to make something of it – our essence. The meaning that we get in our lives comes from within and not from without. There are no divine guidelines or solutions. You need to understand carefully what I am saying here, for, as a full-time educator, I am certainly not saying that we must do it all for ourselves or that every human being must start from scratch. We can certainly learn from and build on the efforts and successes of others. I didn't have to go out and discover evolutionary theory. But the overall sense that I make from it is mine and from me, not from others and certainly not from God Almighty. If I save a child from drowning, it is because I want to do so, not because God tells me to do so. I cannot hide behind anyone's skirts, certainly not His.

Humans As Social

So what do I want to say about human nature? What is it that we work within and through to express our essence? Above all, that we are social. One reads about hermits, but mainly because they are so very atypical. Humans work and flourish because they are parts of groups. The great metaphysical poet John Donne, dean of St Paul's in the early seventeenth century, knew this full well.

> No man is an island entire of itself; every man
> is a piece of the continent, a part of the main;
> if a clod be washed away by the sea, Europe
> is the less, as well as if a promontory were, as
> well as any manner of thy friends or of thine
> own were; any man's death diminishes me,
> because I am involved in mankind.
> And therefore never send to know for whom
> the bell tolls; it tolls for thee.
> (John Donne, MEDITATION XVII, Devotions upon
>   Emergent Occasions)

Aristotle was there long before. It is not exclusively a Christian sentiment. Writing in his *Nicomachean Ethics*, he stated that:

> [Friendship] is either itself a virtue or connected with virtue; and next it is a thing most necessary for life, since no one would choose to live without friends though he should have all the other good things in the world: and, in fact, men who are rich or possessed of authority and influence are thought to have special need of friends: for where is the use of such prosperity if there be taken away the doing of kindnesses of which friends are the most usual and most commendable objects? Or how can it be kept or preserved without friends? because the greater it is so much the more slippery and hazardous: in poverty moreover and all other adversities men think friends to be their only refuge. (1998, Chap. VIII)

Guided by Charles Darwin's favorite principle, the Rule of Three, I suggest that our sociality falls into three main categories. First, family. I mean here one's parents, one's partner or partners (in some societies like the nineteenth-century Mormons), one's siblings, one's children, and then out through various more distant relatives – uncles, aunts, cousins, nieces, nephews, and so forth. Sexual desires and activities are very important. John Donne again:

> Licence my roving hands, and let them go,
> Before, behind, between, above, below.
> O my America! my new-found-land,
> My kingdom, safeliest when with one man mann'd,
> My Mine of precious stones, My Empirie,

How blest am I in this discovering thee!
To enter in these bonds, is to be free;
Then where my hand is set, my seal shall be.
Full nakedness! All joys are due to thee
                    ("To his mistress going to bed")

Notwithstanding adolescent fantasies, most of married life is not having sexual intercourse. It is intense. Raising children, working to support the family, caring for the sick and helping the young and less fortunate. All very social and so very human. And totally backed by biology. Survival and reproduction is what it is all about. I am not at all saying that someone without children, especially deliberately without children, cannot have a full and satisfying life. I am saying they are missing something at the heart of being human. Why on earth else would you put up with teenagers?

Second, we have our places and roles in society. Going to school or college or university. Getting a job. Buying a house and getting work done on it. Going to the stores. Using transport, public or otherwise. Paying taxes. Going on vacation. And everything else. When you think about it, biologically humans are sissies. We are not very strong or fast. My four-month-old Cairn terrier can way outrun me or any other human. We are not very well clad. Again, my terrier is simply unaware of cold and rain, when I am shivering and blue despite my clothing. We are prone to all sorts of physical issues, starting with childbirth and our initial helplessness. (In truth, I cannot pretend that my Cairn terrier has starred at the canine equivalent of potty training.)

So how do we succeed? By helping others and by being helped by others. Schoolteachers, professors, doctors, realtors, Airbnb, bus drivers, pilots, civil servants, shopkeepers, and all the rest. No real secret here. I help you. You help me. I scratch your back. You scratch mine. It is known in the trade as "reciprocal altruism." Truly, it is more like an insurance scheme. I throw my help into the general pool, and as needed I withdraw from the general pool. There are going to be cheaters but there always are, and we have many good biological detection mechanisms. We soon spot and disapprove of the person not pulling their weight. Morality is an important adaptation here. We don't spend our time calculating the risks and benefits. We get on with the job because we sense that it is right – it is the morally correct thing to do. Sometimes this intuition will backfire. Not much from the pool for the wretched soldier going over the top in the First World War. But, to quote the last line from *Some Like It Hot*, when Jack Lemmon reveals to his fiancé that he is a guy in girl's clothing: "Nobody's perfect." No system exists without kinks. (It is interesting that, when the squaddie goes over the top to face near-certain death, he does it not from duty or the call of king and country. Perhaps partly in fear of the consequences of not so doing but mainly because he doesn't want to let down his mates. The more you can relate directly to fellow humans, the more important it is.)

And, so, to the third aspect of human sociality. Here I refer to culture broadly construed – religion, arts, sports, literature, cuisine, and so the list grows. Is it biologically adaptive or is it what Stephen Jay Gould called an "exaptation," something on the top of adaptations but not in itself adaptive? I am not sure and I am not sure it matters hugely. Clearly some things are adaptive, cuisine, for instance. Herding animals and then cooking them opened up huge possibilities for successful living and reproduction. Playing baseball rather than cricket? I know that people make religions of their sports – I teach at a football-obsessed institution, where the coach gets paid at least ten times the president – but given the damage that particular activity does to the bodies and brains of young people, I cannot imagine its adaptive value is high. Although, given the sexual misdemeanors of star quarterbacks – again I speak somewhat self-referentially about my own institution – perhaps biologically I take too pessimistic a view on this.

The point is that culture is hugely social. Religion is all about people getting together in groups. "For where two or three are gathered together in my name, there am I in the midst of them" (Matthew 18:20). The arts? Painting is again and again representing people together, and a still life is about things collected and placed by people. One of my all-time favorite paintings, in the National Gallery of Scotland, is an early Vermeer – "Christ in the house of Martha and Mary." It is religious, of course, but for me it is the love being shown, for Jesus, by those two young women. It is not sexual, but it is truly spiritual. Not just adoration, but genuine love of one human being – two in this case – for another. And yet concern and pity and pride, sensing the agony to come and the integrity that this would demand and evince.

As one continues on through the list, sociality predominates. Sports are all about being with other people – and often, having other people watch. Literature likewise. It is true that there are some novels about solitary people, Robinson Crusoe for a start and William Golding's *Pincher Martin*, about a man shipwrecked on a rock in the Atlantic, for a second. But they are still social. Crusoe spends the first half of the novel using the skills he learned from his culture back home, and the second half relating to the savage he protects, Man Friday. *Pincher Martin* is odd, because it turns out at the end of the novel that the protagonist is dead from the beginning. It is the doppelgänger that is the central figure of the story, and it is highly social (in a rather asocial way!) as it works through the bad relationships of Martin during his life. (Golding was for a while an enthusiast for the thought of Rudolf Steiner, and Steiner had this theory that at death the doppelgänger separates from the person and then decays and dies after working through the bad aspects of the person. The still-living true being is thus cleansed and ready for another incarnation. I am just explaining this folks, not accepting it.)

Finally, cuisine. You hardly need to be a gourmand to know what a social activity this is. From pizza parties to state dinners with the queen or the president. When I was younger, I used to spend weeks away in archives, looking at unpublished material on and around evolutionary biology. I loved doing that – and it wasn't just because I could get away from the kids – but I hated the evenings when all was closed. I simply could not go to a proper restaurant on my own. I ate more Big Macs on these trips than was at all decent. And Dunkin Donuts? My home from home. In England? Lots of fish and chips, eaten on park benches, while I read the greasy copies, in which they were wrapped, of the banned-at-my-boarding-school *News of the World*. Hence my detailed knowledge of naughty vicars.

I do want to make clear that although, in a very important way, my whole approach to human nature is "holistic," in the sense that I want to integrate us into society or societies, I am not doing this because I am committed to a philosophy of holism, as something good in itself. (As in the "holistic" pet kibble my wife is conned into buying for our dogs.) I am rather wary of holism as a general philosophy. The biggest holists of the twentieth century were the National Socialists: *Ein Volk, Ein Reich, Ein Führer.* I think you can be a reductionist and a holist at the same time. My biological approach is strictly selfish-gene based, as is the approach of almost all evolutionary biologists today. It is just that I think an individual-selectionist approach can handle group situations readily. Darwin showed that in the *Descent of Man*. Kin selection, reciprocal altruism, and the like yield organisms working together for mutual benefit. I recognize that because of their culture, humans in some sense can transcend their biology, but only in a certain limited fashion. Here, I am right with Edward O. Wilson – and I suspect near all evolutionary biologists – when he said that genes hold culture on a leash.

And the World Said

There you have my own personal approach to the monotheism and atheism question. I am not a monotheist. I am not a theist. Although I hate aspects of religion – the Methodists refusing to accept gay and lesbian ministers, Catholic priests feeling up the pants of little boys, flying planes into the World Trade Center – I do not think religion all bad, neither do I think religious people are all fools or knaves. I am a nonbeliever. An atheist certainly about much in monotheism. I do not think a Creator God stands behind everything that the Western monotheists – Jews, Christians, Muslims – identify as the cause. The answer to why is there something rather than nothing. I am not very keen on resurrections either, although I do concede that something rather marvelous might have happened to those disciples on the third day. Entirely natural, however. I am keen on science – I am a fanatical Darwinian – but I do not accept scientism. I think there are genuine questions that science cannot answer and probably never will answer. Why is there something rather than nothing? Is there an ultimate basis for ethics? What is the true connection between mind and body? What does it all mean? Religion can try to answer these questions, although I don't think it is always very successful or helpful. However, in this sense, I am an accommodationist, thinking that science and religion can exist side by side. It all comes down to faith in a way. I don't have faith, and I doubt the reason is that I am tainted by original sin in a way that Franklin Graham and other Christian bigwigs are not. Am I – and Richard Dawkins and Dan Dennett and Sam Harris and Christopher Hitchens and Ed Wilson and the whole bunch of them – truly corrupted by something done by Adam, in a way not true of Cardinal Pell, the Australian prelate – apparently the previous Number Three in the Vatican – convicted of ejaculating into the mouths of naughty choir boys?

I am an agnostic or skeptic. I leave you with the wise words of British population geneticist J. B. S. Haldane. "My own suspicion is that the Universe is not only queerer than we suppose, but queerer than we can suppose" (1927, 286). The important thing for me, as an existentialist, is not to regret this, but to seize it as an opportunity to live life as a human being to the full. That means being at one with your fellow human beings – Cairn terriers sometimes too! The only truly happy person is the person giving to others. Not a bad note on which to end this Element.

References

Aristotle. 1998. *Nicomachean Ethics*. Editor J. A. Smith. Mineola, NY: Dover.

Augustine. 1982. *The Literal Meaning of Genesis*. Translator J. H. Taylor. New York: Newman.

1998. *Confessions*. Translator H. Chadwick. Oxford: Oxford University Press.

Boyle, R. [1688]1966. A Disquisition about the Final Causes of Natural Things. *The Works of Robert Boyle*. 6 vols. Editor T. Birch, 5:392–444. Hildesheim: Georg Olms.

Bullivant, S. B. and M. Ruse, editors. 2013. *Oxford Handbook to Atheism*. Oxford: Oxford University Press.

Camus, A. [1942]1955. *The Myth of Sysiphus*. London: Hamish Hamilton.

Coyne, J. A. 2015. *Faith Versus Fact: Why Science and Religion Are Incompatible*. New York: Viking.

Crane, T. 2017. *The Meaning of Belief: Religion from an Atheist's Point of View*. Cambridge, MA: Harvard University Press.

Darwin, C. 1859. *On the Origin of Species by Means of Natural Selection, or The Preservation of Favoured Races in the Struggle for Life*. London: John Murray.

1871. *The Descent of Man, and Selection in Relation to Sex*. London: John Murray.

1958. *The Autobiography of Charles Darwin, 1809–1882*. Editor N. Barlow. London: Collins.

1985–. *The Correspondence of Charles Darwin*. Cambridge: Cambridge University Press.

Dawkins, R. 1976. *The Selfish Gene*. Oxford: Oxford University Press.

1983. Universal Darwinism. *Evolution from Molecules to Men*. Editor D. S. Bendall, 403–425. Cambridge: Cambridge University Press.

1986. *The Blind Watchmaker*. New York: Norton.

2006. *The God Delusion*. New York: Houghton, Mifflin, Harcourt.

Dennett, D. C. 2006. *Breaking the Spell: Religion As a Natural Phenomenon*. New York: Viking.

Dickens, C. [1850]1948. *David Copperfield*. Oxford: Oxford University Press.

Dijksterhuis, E. J. 1961. *The Mechanization of the World Picture*. Oxford: Oxford University Press.

Dostoevsky, F. [1879–1880]2003. *The Brothers Karamazov*. London: Penguin.

Franklin, B. 2009. *Autobiography*. Oxford: Oxford University Press.

Gould, S. J. 1999. *Rocks of Ages: Science and Religion in the Fullness of Life*. New York: Ballantine.

Haldane, J. B. S. 1927. *Possible Worlds and Other Essays*. London: Chatto and Windus.

Hall, A. R. 1954. *The Scientific Revolution 1500–1800: The Formation of the Modern Scientific Attitude*. London: Longman, Green and Company.

Hardy, T. 1994. *Collected Poems*. Ware, Hertfordshire: Wordsworth Poetry Library.

Harris, S. 2004. *The End of Faith: Religion, Terror, and the Future of Reason*. New York: Free Press.

Haught, J. F. 2008. *God and the New Atheism: A Critical Response to Dawkins, Harris, and Hitchens*. Louisville, KY: Westminster John Knox Press.

Hick, J. 1973. *God and the Universe of Faiths: Essays in the Philosophy of Religion*. New York: St. Martin's Press.

  2005. *An Autobiography*. London: Oneworld Publications.

Hitchens, C. 2007. *God Is Not Great: How Religion Poisons Everything*. New York: Hachette.

Hume, D. [1757]1963. A Natural History of Religion. *Hume on Religion*. Editor R. Wollheim, 31–98. London: Fontana.

  [1739–1740]1978. *A Treatise of Human Nature*. Oxford: Oxford University Press.

Hutton, J. 1788. Theory of the Earth; or An Investigation of the Laws Observable in the Composition, Dissolution, and Restoration of Land upon the Globe. *Transactions of the Royal Society of Edinburgh* 1, no. 2: 209–304.

Huxley, J. S. 1927. *Religion without Revelation*. London: Ernest Benn.

Ingersoll, R. G. 1874. *The Gods and Other Lectures*. Peoria, IL: Privately Printed.

John Paul II. 1998. *Fides et Ratio: Encyclical Letter of John Paul II to the Catholic Bishops of the World*. Vatican City: L'Osservatore Romano.

Kepler, J. 1977. *The Harmony of the World*. Translators E. J. Aiton, A. M. Duncan, and J. V. Field. Philadelphia, PA: American Philosophical Society.

Kitcher, P. 2014. *Life after Faith: The Case for Secular Humanism*. New Haven, CT: Yale University Press.

Kuhn, T. 1993. Metaphor in Science. In *Metaphor and Thought*. 2nd edn. Editor A. Ortony, 533–542. Cambridge: Cambridge University Press.

Lakoff, G. and Johnson M. 1980. *Metaphors We Live By*. Chicago, IL: University of Chicago Press.

Larson, E. J. 1997. *Summer for the Gods: The Scopes Trial and America's Continuing Debate over Science and Religion*. New York: Basic Books.

LeDrew, S. 2016. *The Evolution of Atheism: The Politics of a Modern Movement*. New York: Oxford University Press.

Leibniz, G. F. W. 1714. *Monadology and other Philosophical Essays*. New York: Bobbs-Merrill.

Lewis, C. S. 1955. *Surprised by Joy: The Shape of My Early Life*. London: Geoffrey Bles.

Lucretius. 1950. *Of the Nature of Things*. translator W. E. Leonard. London: Dutton (Everyman's Library).

Lyell, C. 1830–1833. *Principles of Geology: Being an Attempt to Explain the Former Changes in the Earth's Surface by Reference to Causes now in Operation*. London: John Murray.

Marrin, A. 1974. *The Last Crusade: The Church of England in the First World War*. Durham, NC: Duke University Press.

Marx, K. 1844. A Contribution to the Critique of Hegel's Philosophy of Right Introduction. *Deutsch-Französische Jahrbücher*, February 7 and 10.

McGrath, A. and J. C. McGrath. 2007. *The Dawkins Delusion? Atheist Fundamentalism and the Denial of the Divine*. Downers Grove, IL: InterVarsity Press.

Myers, F. W. H. 1881. G. Eliot. *The Century Magazine*: November, 47.

Newman, J. H. 1973. *The Letters and Diaries of John Henry Newman, XXV*. Editors C. S. Dessain and T. Gornall. Oxford: Clarendon Press.

Noll, M. 2002. *America's God: From Jonathan Edwards to Abraham Lincoln*. New York: Oxford University Press.

Numbers, R. L. 2006. *The Creationists: From Scientific Creationism to Intelligent Design*. Standard edn. Cambridge, MA: Harvard University Press.

Paley, W. [1802]1819. *Natural Theology (Collected Works: IV)*. London: Rivington.

Pennock, R. 1998. *Tower of Babel: Scientific Evidence and the New Creationism*. Cambridge, MA: MIT Press.

Porterfield, A. 2012. *Conceived in Doubt: Religion and Politics in the New American Nation (American Beginnings, 1500–1900)*. Chicago, IL: University of Chicago Press.

Richards, R. J. and M. Ruse. 2016. *Debating Darwin*. Chicago, IL: University of Chicago Press.

Ruse, M. 1979. *The Darwinian Revolution: Science Red in Tooth and Claw*. Chicago, IL: University of Chicago Press.

1986. *Taking Darwin Seriously: A Naturalistic Approach to Philosophy.* Oxford: Blackwell.

1988b. *Homosexuality: A Philosophical Inquiry.* Oxford: Blackwell.

1996. *Monad to Man: The Concept of Progress in Evolutionary Biology.* Cambridge, MA: Harvard University Press.

2001. *Can a Darwinian Be a Christian? The Relationship between Science and Religion.* Cambridge: Cambridge University Press.

2010. *Science and Spirituality: Making Room for Faith in the Age of Science.* Cambridge: Cambridge University Press.

2012. *The Philosophy of Human Evolution.* Cambridge: Cambridge University Press.

2013. *The Gaia Hypothesis: Science on a Pagan Planet.* Chicago, IL: University of Chicago Press.

2015. *Atheism: What Everyone Needs to Know.* Oxford: Oxford University Press.

2017. *On Purpose.* Princeton, NJ: Princeton University Press.

2018. *The Problem of War: Darwinism, Christianity, and Their Battle to Understand Human Conflict.* Oxford: Oxford University Press.

2019. *A Meaning to Life.* Oxford: Oxford University Press.

Ruse, M., editor. 1988a. *But Is It Science? The Philosophical Question in the Creation/Evolution Controversy.* Buffalo, NY: Prometheus.

Ruse, M. and R. J. Richards, editors. 2017. *The Cambridge Handbook of Evolutionary Ethics.* Cambridge: Cambridge University Press.

Ruse, M. and E. O. Wilson. 1986. Moral Philosophy As Applied Science. *Philosophy* 61: 173–192.

Russell, B. 1927. *Why I Am Not a Christian.* London: Watts.

St. Anselm. 1903. *Anselm: Proslogium, Monologium, an Appendix on Behalf of the Fool by Gaunilon; and Cur Deus Homo.* Editor S. N. Deane. Chicago, IL: Open Court.

St. T. Aquinas. 1952. *Summa Theologica, I.* London: Burns, Oates and Washbourne.

1975. *Summa Contra Gentiles.* Translator V. J. Bourke. Notre Dame, IN: University of Notre Dame Press.

Sartre, J. P. 1948. *Existentialism and Humanism.* Brooklyn, NY: Haskell House Publishers Ltd.

Spencer, H. 1857. Progress: Its Law and Cause. *Westminster Review* 67: 244–267.

Weinberg, S. 1977. *The First Three Minutes: A Modern View of the Origin of the Universe.* New York: Basic Books.

Whitcomb, J. C. and H. M. Morris. 1961. *The Genesis Flood: The Biblical Record and Its Scientific Implications*. Philadelphia, PA: Presbyterian and Reformed Publishing Company.

Wilson, E. O. 1975. *Sociobiology: The New Synthesis*. Cambridge, MA: Harvard University Press.

1978. *On Human Nature*. Cambridge, MA: Harvard University Press.

2006. *The Creation: A Meeting of Science and Religion*. New York: Norton

Religion and Monotheism

Paul K. Moser

Loyola University Chicago

Paul K. Moser is Professor of Philosophy at Loyola University Chicago. He is the author of *The God Relationship; The Elusive God* (winner of a national book award from the Jesuit Honor Society); *The Evidence for God; The Severity of God; Knowledge and Evidence* (all Cambridge University Press); and *Philosophy after Objectivity* (Oxford University Press); co-author of *Theory of Knowledge* (Oxford University Press); editor of *Jesus and Philosophy* (Cambridge University Press) and *The Oxford Handbook of Epistemology* (Oxford University Press); and co-editor of *The Wisdom of the Christian Faith* (Cambridge University Press). He is the co-editor with Chad Meister of the book series *Cambridge Studies in Religion, Philosophy, and Society.*

Chad Meister

Bethel University

Chad Meister is Professor of Philosophy and Theology and Department Chair at Bethel University. He is the author of *Introducing Philosophy of Religion* (Routledge, 2009); *Christian Thought: A Historical Introduction*, 2nd edition (Routledge, 2017); and *Evil: A Guide for the Perplexed*, 2nd edition (Bloomsbury, 2018). He has edited or co-edited the following: *The Oxford Handbook of Religious Diversity* (Oxford University Press, 2010); *Debating Christian Theism* (Oxford University Press, 2011), with Paul Moser; *The Cambridge Companion to the Problem of Evil* (Cambridge University Press, 2017); and, with Charles Taliaferro, *The History of Evil* (Routledge, 2018, in six volumes).

About the Series

This Cambridge Element series publishes original concise volumes on monotheism and its significance. Monotheism has occupied inquirers since the time of the biblical patriarchs, and it continues to attract interdisciplinary academic work today. Engaging, current, and concise, the Elements benefit teachers, researchers, and advanced students in religious studies, biblical studies, theology, philosophy of religion, and related fields.

Cambridge Elements ☰

Religion and Monotheism

Elements in the Series

Printed in the United States
By Bookmasters